Spirituality

A LIFE FORCE

Christine A Adams

Copyright

Third Edition Reprint

Copyright© 2019 Christine A Adams

ISBN 13: 978-1-7331986-5-3

Published by Hanley-Adams Publishing – 2019

Human Authored™, Reg #: 1131035,

https://authorsguild.org/human

All rights reserved.

Second Edition- Reprint

Copyright@2017 Christine A Adams

ISBN: 10 154052595

ISBN 13: 978-1540525291

Published by Christine A. Adams - 2017

All rights reserved. No part of this book may be reproduced or utilized in any form or by any means, electronic or mechanical, including photo-copying, recording or by any information storage or retrieval system, without permission in writing from the publisher.

Table of Contents

Chapter 1	1
Chapter 2	25
Chapter 3	45
Chapter 4	61
Chapter 5	87
Chapter 6	111
Chapter 7	133
Chapter 8	161
Chapter 9	179
About the Author	203
Also by Christine A. Adams	205
Living In Love	207
Introduction	209
Chapter 1 - You Are A Child Of God	217

Chapter 1

Spiritual Teaching

A special teacher--everyone seems to have a "special teacher" story! My story started in the seventh grade with Mrs. Parsons, the most loving teacher I ever had. Ironically, I remember her being especially well dressed.

I wondered how she got everything to match so well? Or is it good? "Well" and "good." She told us something about those words. Well, anyway her shoes and her belt match, and it's just the right color to go with her beige skirt and sweater. She's matched up like that, not just once a week, but every day. Today she's sitting on the radiator by the window watching us finish our test.

Diagramming sentences. It's getting so hard. I think this sentence has double or triple gerund phrases. Oh! Oh! Here she comes!

"When you finish, Christine. You and your cast can go out in the hall to rehearse."

"Alright, Mrs. Parsons."

I loved the idea of having my own cast of players so I put down three parallel lines and joined them with a dotted line, put my paper on the desk and gave the signal to Jimmy and Peggy.

Christine A. Adams

This week we would do a crazy play called "Who Put The Overalls In Mrs. Murphy's Chowder?" It was based on a song that came straight from Ireland just like my mother, Bridget McKenna. I hope these kids get it!"It" being Irish and all.

Everyone laughed when we were running around the front of the room trying to find out who put the pants in the soup--so I guess the play was a success. Mrs. Parson's stopped laughing long enough to say something about "unusual and different." She always said something nice!

Just then the bell rang. In their rush to get out, some of the kids knocked over the pot and the big spoon we were using for props. Mrs. Parsons helped us pick up the stuff. I told her some of my ideas for next week and she said, "That seems like a good idea, Christine. Why don't you write it up and I'll look at it."

And I've been writing things up ever since. Thirteen books, printed in 24 countries and as many languages. And some place out there in the world there's 2,000,000 separate non-fiction pieces in print that happen to have my name on them. It all began when she said, "Christine, why don't you write it up?"

But we did a lot more than silly little plays those years. I was fortunate enough to get Mrs. Parsons for English for three years. They moved her up and somehow she kept getting our class. She made sure I understood the "well" and "good" thing, diagrammed more tough sentences, and studied Shakespeare's **Merchant of Venice.**

Mrs. Parsons had this kind of tricky learning. You got a "contract" and decided how much work you would do and what your grade would be. Everyone would try to get an A and we all put together this Globe theatre thing. But we learned!

I learned so much in those years that English became my favorite subject in high school, I majored in English in College, and got my Master's in British Literature. Then, I went right out in the world and taught British Literature to high school seniors for 32 years. Just like Mrs. Parsons, the same old thing, diagramming sentences, Shakespeare and contracts! Some of my students even became English teachers like me.

But there's more than English to the Mrs. Parson's story. There was something about the way she cared for everyone. Her sense of fairness was just like her matching outfits--the same all the way around. It didn't matter if life was hard for you, or if you were poor, she loved you just the way you were. Simply put, she had a way of loving and valuing you until you could love yourself. She did it by teaching you what she was and what you were to her!

She was awfully busy in those days loving and caring for so many kids. It was like they were her own huge family and she wanted them to make it in the world. She set a high standard for herself and for us. We noticed! We listened!

During my freshman year, which was my last year with Mrs. Parson's, my father died and my mother was left with eight kids from ages two to fifteen. We didn't hear many Irish songs around our house any more. But Mrs. Parsons helped me find my way through that painful year. Then, she continued to help my brothers and sisters as they came along. These were discouraging times but she always cared and held us to a high standard. Again simply put, she loved and valued us until we could love ourselves.

One thing about Mrs. Parsons, she was tough. She never gave up on us. We all tested her, each one of us in a new and different way. Sometimes she was the last ally on the playing field.

We're all a little older these days. Now, I can call Mrs. Parsons, "Jenny". She is still my inspiration, my teacher and my friend. Some days we talk about teaching English with an excitement that only two former English teachers can muster up. We talk about how great it was to be a teacher, and tell stories about "our school kids." Some days we talk of memories of my youth, or her youth. Some days we just talk about life. But we never run out of things to talk about.

And when I tell her I have an idea for a new book, she keeps saying to me, "Christine, why don't you write that up?" And I do. Things haven't changed much really. I still love and admire her now just as I did then. Sometimes I remember the day the class laughed about the overalls in Mrs. Murphy's chowder and the tone of her voice when she said "unusual and different." And I think how strange it is that I remember the tone of her voice?

When I think of her tone of voice, I remember to tell her, "You are the reason my life began to take form--back in the seventh grade, and continues moving forward today. You were my best teacher!"

But what is a good teacher?

In the eyes of the world we think of good teachers as the ones who give special information to "learners." That special learning might be an area of the teacher's expertise: math, language arts, physics, science--areas of expertise that pertain to a body of knowledge within the physical world. In that sense and on those occasions, the teacher does impart special information to the learner.

Yet almost everyone has a Mrs. Parsons story like mine. A story of someone who reached beyond the body of knowledge in some spiritual way. The teaching might not have occurred in a classroom setting. The teacher might have been a family member, a friend or even a stranger.

It was someone who provided an inspiring example to the learner; someone who believed in themselves first and then transferred that belief to the student and encouraged them. That is really why these teachers are remembered--not for the grammar, the equations, the formulas they taught or situations of life they shared with you. They are remembered for the love they showed.

When love and caring are involved, a new kind of teacher emerges and the lesson is spiritual. The student learns to love by the example of love given. These teachers become spiritual teachers of love, or "Teachers of God."

Of course, I followed in Mrs. Parson's footsteps and became an English teacher. I tried to live up to her example and the learner became the teacher--literally. In following a teaching profession, I had plenty of opportunities to show love for my students and many times my students, the learners, became my teacher.

Each year as I started my school year, inevitably, there would be a boy or girl who was so starved for love that they became a discipline problem to get attention. They would be abusive in language, loud, and unruly; therefore, they became the first to report to the principal's office.

I remember Billy, a tall good looking senior, who appeared to be tough and mean. Billy had disruption down to a science! There were interruptions, burping in class, side comments and faces in his repertoire. I complied with his wishes for attention and sent him directly to the principal's office.

On the third trip, he divulged this information as he left the room, "Just trying to break my record. Last year's English teacher threw me out thirty-three times." I thought about that and decided to stop throwing him out. I began "to teach only love."

When he was abusive, I went up to him and in a loving voice corrected him. He didn't know what to do with the love. This might have been the first time anyone treated him that way.

As the year progressed, the situation got better when Billy was allowed to read Stephen King in an independent reading program. He devoured the books and remained quiet in class. When I went to The American Bookseller's Convention that year, I told Stephen King's publisher about Billy and he sent copies of his latest books. Billy was impressed!

The turning point came when I did a positive affirmations exercise with the class. Each student was supposed to list ten positive things about another student. No one picked Billy! So, I made up his list! He watched me write: 1. tall 2. good-looking 3. nice smile 4. dark hair 5. loyal 6. persistent 7. loves to read 8. beautiful face 9. dark eyes 10. never forgets. When I was done, he smiled and said, "How did you know that stuff." I said, "I just know, Billy." Teaching is not all English-- it's love.

Spirituality: A Life Force

It was true Billy was a terrible student--ill disciplined, aggravating, rude, and disrespectful. But I asked God to let me see him differently through the eyes of love rather than fear. By changing my perspective of him, I changed his of himself. It's like that--love generates love.

We give love to others so that we can remain at peace within ourselves. I didn't let Billy run rampant over the class as we did the typical test of authority in the early days of the class. Then, when it was appropriate, I switched and let love in--not out of weakness but out of strength. There's the difference. So many people think it's weak to be defenseless but, at appropriate times, defenselessness shows great power. Teaching love looks passive sometimes but it generates a lasting energy.

A child of God is a "teacher of God."

I first encountered the term, "A Teacher of God", in reading *A Course In Miracles.* Before that time, I believed that Sister Theresa, Gandhi or the Dali Lama might fit that description but not the ordinary person.

Then, as I continued to read *The Course* and write about love in *Living In Love*, published in 1993 by Health Communications, Inc., I began to understand that we all are teachers. Whether we know it or not, we all teach what we are. If we believe that God is Love, and that we are of God; then we teach only Love. In that spiritual sense we are "Teachers of God."

The teacher and learner are the same!

Another concept that baffled me at first was the notion that the teacher and learner are the same. How could that be? I always saw the teacher as the leader imparting some special information to the learner--using the worldly definition of teaching. However, as we learn, we teach by showing what we are.

Let's look at teaching as a demonstration. **The Course** describes two thought systems: one governed by the ego and the material world of illusions and the other governed by the spirit. It makes sense that if you choose the spiritual path, you will teach what you are learning, as a matter of fact; you will witness to attest what you believe. In that sense the teacher and the learner are the same.

"In this sense spiritual teaching is not done by words alone. It is done through every situation of your life which becomes a chance to teach others what you are and what they are to you. No more than that, but never less!" (ACIM)

Examples of spiritual teaching!

Parenting affords us the opportunity to teach what we are and to demonstrate to our children what they are to us. The world can be falling down around the child but as long as there are parental examples of love and courage, the learning is going on.

In recounting my childhood in an unpublished autobiographical work entitled **The Chokecherry Tree,** I wrote of a time of great significance--the end of World War 11. As important as the war was in my memory, even more significant was the night of the birth of my brother, David.

1945 -- The End of World War 11-- and the Birth of David

Then it happened! President Franklin Delano Roosevelt died. I guess he hadn't been well for quite a while. A man named Harry Truman became president. People worried about the war effort and what would happen in America. Everyone was very sad when F.D.R. died. It was like the whole world turned dark overnight.

Suddenly, a short time later, that darkness lifted when the war ended in 1945. There were stories about people dancing in the streets, and newspaper pictures of soldiers and sailors kissing girls. Everything seemed brand new. Shining--like the buttons on the soldiers uniforms.

Bridie McKenna, my mother, was due to have a new child. On the night the sixth child, David, was born, it snowed. The whiteness began to collect on the windows in the kitchen. The driveway filled up, the front porch steps were slippery.

When Mike came home from work he realized they were in for a terrible nor'easter so he shoveled out the driveway before supper. "I've had a little pain, off and on," she said as they sat down to supper. The corn beef and cabbage was piled in a dish in the middle of the table. Steam rose into the air. The butter was on a long narrow dish beside the bread.

Christine A. Adams

Mike knew it might be a long night so he ate heartily. The kids ran around the kitchen table playing together. "Mommy, Michael is hitting us," the girls reported to their weary mother.

"Mike" she answered directing the question to her weary husband. Mike reluctantly left his food and went into the living room to straighten out the kids. He put Danny in his playpen, gave Michael a puzzle and Raymond some trucks to play with and sent the girls to their rooms to do their homework.

"Michael you keep an eye on Raymond and Danny, and have that puzzle done by the time I come back," he said sternly to his son. A break in the noise ensued. There was a secret kind of signal that came over the house when their father "straightened out the kids". They all knew this was no time to disobey.

"What if I have to go tonight," she said touching her stomach.

"We'll make it. I'll put the chains on now so as to be ready. We'll put the kids down in their clothes and dress them warm, pack em and go. Don't ye worry, Bridie. When it's time. We'll make it!"

Bridie always went to Wyman's Maternity home in Kittery to have the babies. There she would meet Doctor Shapleigh who delivered all the McKenna's. Tonight she was worried about the seven mile ride to Kittery.

Later that night, Bridie's water broke and she woke Mike to tell him it would be "soon". No one quite knew what "soon" meant but it did mean you'd better find your boots and mittens and put them on as fast as you can, and then find your brothers boots and mittens and pull them over their hands and feet as quick as you can.

Spirituality: A Life Force

The snow swirled around the car and the windshield wipers beat at the windows. It was like being in a tunnel where there was no end just white swirling snow. My sister and I each had one brother glued to us sandwiched in the back seat with Danny, the youngest, in the middle. He was drinking a bottle and making noises to try to get back to sleep.

Michael and Raymond finally drifted off under the crock of a sister's arm. Bridie was making noises in the front seat. No one talked. The snow seemed to drive the car back. There were no other cars on the road. Mike drove on persistently. The chains clanked together. There was a bridge, a streetlight, some telephone poles and the constant wind and snow.

Bridie broke the silence with a louder noise. Then hardly breathing she said, "Mike, I don't know." We didn't know what she didn't know but we knew it was serious. The boys slept, Danny stirred and shifted in his seat. Everyone moved to fit him in.

Mike drove the car on through the snow until he saw the sign Wyman's. There was a steep unplowed hill up to Wyman's and he knew the car wouldn't go up that hill. He stopped at the bottom of the driveway and quickly went to Bridie in the front seat. She tried to struggle out of the door and couldn't move.

"I'll have to carry ye, Bridie, don't move. Ye'll hurt the baby. It's the only way. You can't walk."

Too weak to object Bridie leaned against him as he picked her heavy body up and carried her up the hill. Not a word was said to the children in the back seat. No words were needed. We cried quietly. No words just tears of relief. The darkness fell over us like a blanket, the snow gathered on the windshield, it began to get colder. But somehow we were safe and warm, all huddled together.

Something happened that night. Some kind of awareness. Some understanding about birth, and about a woman and a man. It happened when Mike picked Bridie up to carry her up the hill. Somehow when she couldn't help herself, he'd found a way to help her.

That night, in the darkness, in the silent snow, it became very clear to me. You do need men and women to make babies, and to help each other when they can't help themselves. That night, my father's strength and love was the only thing to save her mother, and the new baby, and I knew it!

There is no choice--teaching happens!

On that snowy night my mother and father had no thought of teaching me a lesson. They were simply involved in the constant process of teaching that belongs to being a parent. It's a process that goes on every day, every year, in times of peace, in times of war.

The curriculum that was set up that night was determined by what my mother and father thought they were--parents, husband and wife. The lesson I learned was what I meant to them, how they loved their children and how they loved each other. The lesson was love! They had learned to love and they taught love.

In spiritual teaching, we go to the very heart of the matter. Words are irrelevant. Words may coincide with the teaching but don't have to. What mattered on that snowy night in Maine is that my father picked my mother up and carried her the distance. In

Spirituality: A Life Force

his mind it wasn't too far. She wasn't too heavy. He did it because he loved and believed in her, in the baby, in himself. Spiritual teaching reinforces what you believe about yourself. The self that you believe is real--that is the "self" you teach.

You teach what you think you are!

Just as I proved in my reversal of the "disruptive" Billy in the classroom, it's all about what I believe. If I go through life believing I am vulnerable, limited and weak, I will teach vulnerability, limitedness, and weakness to everyone I meet. If I believe I am a powerful spiritual being, connected to God, A child of God. I will teach that truth.

Think of a time when you were not confident and tried to teach the world you were something you are not. Maybe you tried to show your friends you were something by wearing expensive clothes and driving an expensive car. Did you ever suspect you couldn't do a job but pretended you knew how?

When we don't have a secure spiritual identity, a deep sense of being loved by God, we might pretend we are of this world and teach what we are not. We might teach business executive, professional, lawyer, doctor or Indian Chief. Whatever role we drown ourselves in, it's only a small part of our real identity-- our spiritual identity as a child loved by God.

Earlier in my life I became lost, forgetting the lessons of love taught to me by my parents and Mrs. Parson, sidetracked by material possessions and social status. For a few years, I saw myself only by the roles I played in the world.

Christine A. Adams

My country club years

This was a time in my life when I didn't have a secure spiritual identity--a time when I tried to present an image to the world, a time when I made decisions on appearances. In college, I met and married a man who had all the right credentials: right religion, social and financial status, family business, nationality, and education.

For the first few years we belonged to the "country club set" just as his mother and father had. It really was a phony world of self-aggrandizement, ego-building, and materialism. Both of us were led by our addictions and we drank too much, played too hard, and generally lived on the edge.

Now, when I think of those years I remember how little I had on the inside. It was as if I was spiritually bankrupt. I attended church not to nurture me but to present an image of spirituality to the world. What was I teaching? Status and money! Consistent with my ego-based thinking, I gave back to the world a hollow empty shell of myself.

It was only when the family business failed, and we were financially bankrupt that the country club world came crashing down. Then, I began to grow spiritually. Our friends didn't invite us to their parties anymore--no status, no money. We dropped the country club membership after my husband's 32 years of consecutive "belonging". I went back to work teaching in a local high school. We didn't take our kids to the club pool in summer; we took them camping on an island in the Atlantic Ocean. We canoed the Allagash River instead of going on cruises and no longer felt controlled by the image of status and money. We had freedom to be something else. We didn't know what we would become yet but the door was open to new opportunities.

Many times people say they didn't know "who they were" until striped of all worldly possessions. Some spiritual teachers actually seek to be free of the hindrances of money and position. They seem to have learned that great understanding of self can come through what the materialistic world might consider adversity. I needed to ask myself the biblical question, "What profit is it to a man if he gains the whole world and loses his soul?" (Matthew 16:26 NKJV) When I heard those words spoken in church, I finally understood what they meant?

There are times today that I need to take an inventory and ask myself these questions: What motivates me? What takes up my time? How much of my world is tied to my successes? How much time do I spent promoting myself and worldly interests? What about spiritual interests? How much energy do I expend helping/loving others? Who am I? What do others mean to me? What do I teach?

What is the curriculum of the world?

Whenever anyone is so caught up in their job, earning money, their family traditions or even society itself, they tend to be following the curriculum of the world and tend to teach others what they are not. They are not only the job, the family, the society. These roles are only a small part of our real identity.

"Until you change your mind about who you are and understand your spiritual identity, you will find

yourself teaching a curriculum of the material world which always leads to despair and death." (ACIM)

Working in a public school system for many years gave me the opportunity to get to know thousands of students. They became my teachers. Ironically, the ones with severe disabilities, with the most adversity in their lives, had the most profound lessons to teach. Two incredible examples were Sarah and Josh who had cerebral palsy from birth. I recount their stories here.

A Special Disability :"A CUP OF COFFEE"

The shocking news went through our school like a sudden tremor. It was Sarah, one of the East Conn Kids, the kids who have a special room upstairs. You know, the pretty one who couldn't talk--Sarah was in the cafeteria, with Chris, her aide, holding her hands, typing words on a talking computer. One of the kids asked her what she had always wanted to say and she wrote "F------ you. I'm not stupid!" The kids loved it-- poignantly, powerfully, she made her point with words you don't say in school.

When I heard the story, I cried. Remembering Sarah being lead into the cafe, I thought of her bright colored lunch bag in one hand and the aide holding her firmly with the other. Once, she got away and came and hugged me. I never forgot that gesture. It was like she wanted to reach out of her body and touch someone in the world.

Sarah has Cerebral Palsy, and could not speak, write, communicate with facial expression, or body language, and had only peripheral vision. There didn't seem to be any way to test her cognitive skills so it was assumed they were limited. Many tests had been tried over the years but nothing worked. When they asked Sarah to point to a certain picture, she couldn't hold her hands steady enough to hit the picture.

Consequently, her early education was structured for a person of limited ability: no reading, no writing, spelling--nothing but Sesame Street and the flash cards her mother put up around the house. That's where Sarah was at 14 years of age--no formal education.

The breakthrough came in her freshman year when she began working with Chris, her facilitator, who directed her hands to the computer. She could think, and write thoughts. Then, Sarah was mainstreamed into regular classes with Chris at her side. I anticipated her senior year with eagerness and some trepidation--it would be my turn at having Sarah in my class. When her senior year came, it happened, I scheduled an interview with her and Chris, her aide, who held her hands as she typed. In one of our first sessions, I asked Sarah about what happened the very first time she typed out her first words.

"Who was there?" I asked.

"JOE, CHRIS, ME" The computer spelled out the BIG BLOCK LETTERS that I would come to know as Sarah's distinct voice.

"Why did you try? I questioned.

"I NOT KNOW. I JUST DID. I NOT SURE WHY I TOOK THE CHANCE. OR WHY PEOPLE TOOK THE CHANCE THEY DID BUT I'M GRATEFUL THEY DID."

The letters came out one by one and I felt giddy at being able to speak to the girl who was inside. She had a simple syntax without too much formal sentence structure, sometimes without punctuation, sometimes with misspellings. It was the voice of a child with the limited vocabulary, of one who had been denied direct inter-communication for fourteen years. It was the voice of someone who couldn't speak with her mouth, only her soul. She choose her words carefully. She said only what she meant and she was remarkably wise.

Chris, Sarah's aide, told me that Joe, the speech therapist, had seen demonstrated a new tactic called "facilitation" where an aide holds the hands of the disabled person, somewhat steady, letting them direct their fingers to a keyboard. They tried it because Joe believed Sarah might be able to talk. Joe tested her by asking "What do you want, Sarah?

"What was the first thing you asked for?" I asked eagerly. Somehow I wanted to know exactly what a person might ask for after fourteen years. She told me that when Joe asked her, "What do you want, Sarah?" she spelled out COFFE.

At first Chris and Joe couldn't understand. They thought of coffin or cough, but that didn't work until Chris realized that every day they stopped for coffee and never brought any for Sarah. It was as simple as that--a cup of coffee. Just to be included--one of the gang.

In a subsequent test, Joe removed Sarah from Chris, the facilitator, for a whole day. All day long he taught two words to Sarah--TRUTH AND FAITH. When Chris came to facilitate Sarah, she was unaware of the words taught and Sarah couldn't speak to tell her. Then, Joe prompted Sarah to write the words with Chris holding her hands--and she wrote TRUE. Then came FAITH. This test completed, they knew for sure. It was true! Now Joe had faith! Faith that Sarah had normal intelligence--that she was completely aware even though her body twisted and turned uncontrollably, even though she could only emit ugly sounds, even though she needed to be led when she walked.

Later Sarah wrote on her computer, "I'VE THOUGHT A LOT ABOUT HOW I MIGHT LIVE AND WHERE I BE TODAY IF ANOTHER SOMEBODY HAD BEEN MY AIDE THAT DAY OR IF I HADN'T TRIED. I SORT OF LOOK BACK NOT KNOWING HOW COME I DID TRY. I DO NOT LOOK BACK OFTEN BECAUSE TODAY IT SCARY. I WAS SO SCARED IN THE BEGINNING; I THOUGHT IT WOULD ALL DISAPPEAR. IT TOOK LONG TIME TO REALLY TRUST TO LIVE LIFE, I KEPT THINKING IT MIGHT DISAPPEAR.

As the computer spelled out Sarah's wisdom, I realized my life was being touched with her specialness. The miracle here is that at 19, Sarah earned a 91 average as a member of my regular British Literature class. She graduated with her class after completing a full high school program and even some college courses.

Her resume highlighted her work on the Connecticut's State Disability Boards. Sarah's dream was to finish college and become be an advocate for disabled children. She understood the value of the years she lost and wished to spare others the same fate. My moments with Sarah taught me that you don't need a formal education to speak from the heart, or even the ability to speak, or an extensive vocabulary to touch someone's soul! She did mine. She became my teacher!

Another teacher was Josh.

Josh was also born with cerebral palsy and was not mainstreamed until he was 14. The first time he passed me in the hall I was shocked. The effort it took for him to walk was astounding. His arms were like heavy tree limbs swinging wildly in a windstorm. His head moved aimlessly with his jerky body and he seemed to push his whole body forward with the force of a hurricane. Yet, even with all the physical difficulty there was something wonderful about Josh--his attitude, his spirit.

Because Josh was only a freshman and I taught seniors, our paths didn't cross often but every time I saw him, I felt the presence of his powerful, optimistic spirit. When he spoke, it was as if he had gravel down in his voice box. Sometimes the halting sounds were very long and very harsh but he never failed to speak.

I remember the day he came to my senior class.

Just as the last bell rang, the door opened and Josh kind of flopped in, He made quite an entrance dropping his books on the floor as he fumbled to shut the door.

"SSS S orrr y" he said with a smile that negated the twisted voice of his cerebral palsy. The kids who didn't know Josh laughed and the kids who did know him quietly helped him pick up his books. Josh had been removed from the lower level classes to Level One classes when it was discovered that he was an extremely bright, an avid reader who could compensate for his inability to write by taking oral tests and writing on the computer.

Spirituality: A Life Force

"OK, let's begin. Let's go over the course outline." The fifty-six minute period quickly folded into a twenty-six minute period. When I could see Jake's eyes shutting, I knew that the class had heard enough about British Literature.

"Welcome to your senior year!" Jake head nodded as he heard my words. "OK, this little exercise might help you when you get to your college essays." Again, Jake snapped to attention. The clock hummed an unusually loud hum and Betsy stopped doodling on her notebook.

I explained that everyone has a special talent--a talent that has to be defined. Usually, colleges ask you to write about yourself and your special talents. I explained this as I handed a paper with four questions on it, to the first person in each row. I motioned them to pass it back. They did.

Benjamin had taken out a math book and was starting the first exercise in the book. Quickly, I closed his book, "Only English in this room." Jake seized the moment and borrowed a pencil from Ben.

"Ok, the questions:

1. **What did you love to do as a child?**
2. **Who do you think you are?**
3. **What do you love?**
4. **What could you do and know you would not fail at it?**

5. What is stopping you from pursuing your dreams?"

As the pencils scratched on the paper, Jake wrote about sports and his concern about getting picked for the college draft, Betsy talked about her love of art, her dream of getting into Art School, and her concern that her portfolio would be accepted. Ben recognized his ongoing love of math and science and hoped to be accepted in an engineering program. Jean talked about her writing and how she'd like to major in English. Justin and Jenny showed their answers to each other as they wrote.

Josh laboriously scribbled his answers on his paper bearing down so hard that he almost ripped the paper. His letters were very big and his shaky hands made lines that were squiggly instead of straight. His answers were mostly one word illegible strangulated shapes. I wondered how Josh would ever be able to handle this level one class.

Finally, just before the bell and after the sports, art, and engineering answers from the other kids, I said, "So what do you have, Josh? What did you love to do as a child?"

"Ww-- inn-- tterSs-- k--ing!" came with a smile from his twisted body. The room grew quiet; the clock hummed louder.

"Who do you think you are?"

"Bb-- ussiness – pro-- profess-- ional m--man.

" What do you know you absolutely could not fail at"

Spirituality: A Life Force

"**Ss--k--ingHh--elppp--eoople.**

"What is stopping you from pursuing your goal?"

"**Not--tt--hing!** His smile widened as the bell rang and the kids stacked their papers on the teacher's desk. Jake proudly nudged Josh as he passed by his seat. Josh teetered unsteadily as he acknowledged the nudge and seesawed out the door into the hall.

When Josh was four years old, his parents were told that he'd probably never walk. But Josh kept trying, he walked. Then Josh wanted to learn to ski. Time after time he fell but eventually he skied. Oh, how he skied!

By the time Josh came into my class as a senior, he had become a downhill racer. He attained his Alpine Competitor License and won the Eastern Cup in Alpine racing for two consecutive years. In addition to racing in The National Handicapped Ski Tour, he became a member of the United States Olympic Handicapped Ski Team.

Josh told the press, "When you put your mind to something, you can do it. I don't care what others tell you."

As part of his senior project, he spent time speaking to middle school students about the Special Olympic World Games. During one presentation to a seventh grade class, Josh talked about his experiences traveling with the Olympic Ski Team. He said, "I'm disabled, but I'm an athlete first. When I make my run, my mind says 'athlete, athlete.'"

Josh told me that when he started talking to the younger kids that they were tentative when he first started to speak. "But slowly they warmed up to me. After one presentation, 10 students asked me for my autograph," he added laughing.

Everyone at school became his fan too. The school nurse said, "Nothing stops him, he's not afraid of anything." The secretary in the office said, "He's a role model for a lot of kids. He enlightens them."

Once when asked what a person should do when they meet a disabled person, he said," The most important thing to know is that we're people first and disabled second. And we never give up."

There's something special about someone who speaks, teaches, out of great adversity. We secretly know that what they are saying is "Look at me, I am here, I am right here inside, I am God's child."

Love has a way of extending itself. Just as I was taught love by my parents and Mrs. Parsons, my seventh grade teacher, I was able to love my students. They, in turn, taught me new lessons in love and life and have gone on to lovingly teach others. The circle of spiritual teaching always comes full circle and is never ending.

This book continues to explore spiritual teaching and the spiritual lessons learned. Not everyone you meet teaches you love, but they all teach you a lesson. The question is not whether you will teach for in that there is no choice. Teaching is the constant process which goes on every moment of our day. **The curriculum is set; you teach what you are and what others are to you! So, who are you? What are others to you?**

Chapter 2

A Spiritual Teachers' Characteristics

The qualifications to become a spiritual teacher are very simple. Somehow, somewhere this teacher has made a deliberate choice in which he did not see his interests apart from someone else. Once he has done that the road is established and the spiritual path is clear. It's as if a light has entered that darkness. It may be a single light but that's enough. Because the act of making a deliberate choice where you don't see your interest apart from someone else's, you make an agreement with God--to honor the life of another.

In the following story, Jenny, a brave EMT, gave her life to save others. Therefore, she was honored. Just as Christ gave us salvation through his crucifixion, Jenny became a "bringer of salvation"--a teacher of God. Jennifer was a nurse on the Life Star Helicopter that rescued accident victims and carried them to the Hartford Hospital. One night her helicopter crashed.

Ironically, she was killed trying to rescue someone else! Her death shocked and moved thousands of people. The night of the wake, I stood in line for four hours with thousands of people outside the funeral home. It started to rain. The hundreds of EMT's, firefighters, and policemen took out plastic garbage bags, handed them back through the line and we covered our heads. Lightning flashes cut the sky--it poured. More rain! No one went home--we all stayed in line inching our way into the funeral home. Five thousand of us!

When I finally reached Jennifer's father, a close friend who belonged to my church, and a man of deep faith, he hugged me and said the most remarkable thing, "Some good will come out of this. You will see, Chris. You will see." Even though I could not think of one good thing at the time I answered, "I know, I know."

The next day the memorial service was held at our large city church. Only a fraction of the thousands in attendance could fit into the church. A sound system carried the words of tribute from Jennifer's co-workers to the crowd. Parents whose children had been saved by Jennifer and Life Star wept on the lawn; children whose parents had been saved wept as well. Later, when Jennifer's cremated body was placed in the earth, the Life Star Helicopter passed over the cemetery and everyone wept.

It was difficult to see any logic in Jennifer's death. In her dedication, to die so young, after having been so vital in helping save others--this man's daughter, that man's son, or someone's parent. How could I really agree with her father and see her death as anything good? At that moment, it seemed difficult!

In reflection, I realized she was the most profound example of "a spiritual teacher"--a person who didn't see her interests apart from the victim she saved; a person who made an agreement with God to honor the life of others; a person who gave up her own life trying to save someone else's.

Spirituality: A Life Force

There was a holiness in the outpouring of love at the time of Jennifer's death. Those thousands of EMT's, firefighters, and policemen--those people who work to help others were united in one place, at one time, to honor someone who believed in love and lived in love.

Never could I have recreated a more profound example of "spiritual teaching" than what I saw at Jennifer's funeral. Then, at the internment, when the Life Star Helicopter passed over the gravesite symbolizing that her loving service will continue through those who remained.

At that moment, it was clear that Jennifer's death had great meaning--that she did not die uselessly. Her love went on in the renewed dedication of every service person there. Her love continued on in each mission of that plane, and in each loving act of her colleagues. That was the lesson!

Love is like that--it does not end with the giver. Love flows on to the next person, and the next, and the next. Love brings more love! That was the goodness of her death!

In the first chapter of this book, I described some of my spiritual teachers. Mrs. Parsons, my English teacher, who put my interest above her own and taught me how to teach others. I taught what she taught me to my students and in giving to them, I received many gifts. A pattern emerged in my life. It seems there's a master plan which includes specific contracts to be made by each teacher of God. There are no accidents in salvation. We will meet those who are there to teach us.

How do you recognize a spiritual teacher?

Christine A. Adams

As stated in *A Course In Miracles*, spiritual teachers have ten distinct characteristics: trust, honesty, tolerance, gentleness, joy, defenselessness, generosity, patience, faithfulness, and open-mindedness. We will discuss these characteristics in the remainder of this chapter.

1. TRUST: The first characteristic, trust, provides the foundation for helping teachers function in the world. There are two ways of looking at the world; one, a fearful, uncertain place that is sure to do you in; or two, a safe place where you will be provided for. If you're always on the defensive, you will not have trust. A teacher of God knows in their very being that the world is not governed by its own laws but by a power greater than the world. It's that power that keeps them safe.

After a disastrous divorce, I needed to return to teach high school so that I could support myself. At that time teaching jobs were scarce. So, when I took a job, I was hired as a permanent substitute for three months. If I succeeded in my work, I would be offered a contract in June for the next year. My fears were set in motion when I inherited an unruly class that had to be reined in after having bullied many a "not so permanent substitute."

Every time I prepared to face this class, a wave of fear came over me. They held the key to my survival and I knew it. Everyday right before class, I would read in *A Course In Miracles* meditation entitled, "There is nothing to fear." It states that every time we are afraid we are relying on our own resources, not God's. This reading let me know that the very presence of fear was a sure sign that I was trusting in my own strength. It let me know that when I accepted that "there is nothing to fear," I had gone to that special place in my mind that remembered God and let His strength take the place of my weakness. The moment I was willing to do that, then, indeed there was nothing to fear. The same message came to me in Proverbs 3:56 "Trust in the Lord with all your heart, lean not on your understanding; in all ways acknowledge Him, and He shall direct your path". I trusted in God and I was offered my "life-saving" precious contract in June.

2. HONESTY: All the traits of a teacher of God rest on the first one--trust. Only the trusting person can afford to be honest. If you feel that the world is out to get you, that you're competing to win in the world, and that you'll be harmed by others who're competing to get what you have, you probably won't approach them with honesty.

Honesty implies congruent behavior. Congruence comes when there's nothing you say that contradicts what you think or do, when no thought opposes any other thought, when no act belies your word. Then, you are truly honest! The peace of mind that spiritual teachers ultimately experience is largely due to their perfect honesty.

Being honest with yourself

Sometimes dishonesty comes when we deceive ourselves. We can control situations by interfering with the natural course of events, thinking we have God-like powers. For example, we see ourselves as having the power to change someone else when, in reality, we can only change ourselves. This self-deception brings conflict--self-deception is really dishonesty.

Having the humility to recognize my flawed human nature lead me to my spiritual self. When I was caught up in alcohol addiction, I denied the sickness even though it was apparent to everyone around me. Anyone who is addicted to anything, either a substance or negative behavior, rationalizes and denies. That is self--deceit! We see people in the news who are obviously in trouble with alcohol and drugs. Denial or self-deceit helps them get through the day, protects them, and keeps the addiction going. If they believed they had a problem, they probably would address it. Denial is keeping them from being honest at this time.

Many people lie to themselves with rationalizations. I wouldn't drink if I didn't have all these problems. If only I had a decent childhood; my adult life would be better. If only someone loved me. I have so many problems--no money, no friends, no life--that's why I do what I do.

Honesty can come through failure

A spiritual teacher has learned that their human side is subject to all kinds of human failures but their spiritual side is the strongest and most important part of their being. When pride, or fear of failure, keeps us from recognizing our human frailties, we're not honest. When we can honestly admit failure, we can find spirituality. I found I was able to reach out to God, when I accepted my human frailty.

Although none of us is ever completely aware of our weaknesses, or free from rationalizations, I know for me that the more I'm stripped of pretensions, of secrets I might harbor, of hidden resentments and grievances; I can embrace humility and live an honest life.

3. TOLERANCE: The third characteristic of a spiritual teacher is tolerance. Judgment of others implies a lack of trust and trust is the basis of the teacher of God's whole thought system. When you let trust go--all the learning is gone. By judging others, you assume a position you don't have. Judgment implies you've been deceived in your view of others. If you're deceived in your view of others, you're deceived in your view of yourself.

To judge others is really judging me. I've noticed that I'm the most judgmental when I have the same weakness as the person I'm condemning. How else would I recognize manipulation, for example, if I had not manipulated? So, for me to judge others is to really judge myself. It seems to be a complicated pattern when you judge someone else for your own faults. It's almost as if you publicly denounce the fault so that you might be able to avoid it yourself, and ultimately, bring forgiveness to yourself to relieve the guilt and pain. Harm is caused by judgment. Judging thoughts are harmful thoughts because they really put a verdict of guilt--not on the person being judged, and on oneself.

Judgment of others always brings us to a place of unnatural uneasiness. In the bible we are reminded: "Judge not that you be judged. For with the judgment you pronounce you will be judged, and the measure you give will be the measure you get." Matthew 7:1,2 RSV

In a spiritual sense, it would be difficult to accept that a loving God would make us unequal. So, without judgment all men are brothers, all women sisters. None can stand apart. There are some organized religions that rely heavily on condemnation and judgment to promote their religious beliefs. They self-righteously differentiate--speaking of those who are sinners and those who are "the chosen few." They speak freely of the burden of sin, condemnation of sinners and loss of salvation. Until I was able to rid myself of this heavy burden of self-judgment laid down by many years of religious study, I couldn't accept myself as a loving child of God. And until I was able to internalize the presence of God within, I couldn't find the peace and joy I know today. My tolerance began with me, my forgiveness of others began with forgiveness of myself.

Intolerance of self or others obliterates the teacher's loving function making him confused, fearful, angry and suspicious. No lesson can be learned when there is harmfulness imposed on others. Therefore, God's teachers are wholly gentle.

4. GENTLENESS: The fourth characteristic of a teacher of God is gentleness. Teachers of God need the strength of gentleness. Why Strength? Because when we harm others with our harsh judgment, we are choosing weakness. A gentle world leader, rather than a defiant, bellicose one, stands out for their inner strength.

This truth is often missed by leaders of the world. Martin Luther King, Mahatma Gandhi, Nelson Mandela were gentle spiritual men. In direct contrast, some powerful leaders claim to be spiritual men but defensively initiate war and violence only to end up with a nation confused, fearful, angry and suspicious. President Barak Obama won the Nobel Peace Prize in 2009, not so much because he had brought peace to the world, but because he opened the dialogue for a spirit of cooperation.

Spirituality: A Life Force

Intentionally harming of others makes a person defensive, fearful, and suspicious. When there's harm to others, no spiritual gain can come from it. Although it seems paradoxical, the power of God's teacher lies in their gentleness.

If you believe a loving God is your source of power and that you're connected to the power of God, you'll understand the eternal gentleness of that source. Gentleness means that fear is now impossible--because you are beloved and you are safe in God's Love. Understanding the strength of gentleness in God's Love allows you to extend this gentleness to others. "Be beautiful inside, in your hearts with the lasting charm of a quiet spirit that is so precious to God." 1 Peter 3:4 TLB

5. JOY: Joy, the fifth characteristic of a spiritual teacher, is the inevitable result of gentleness. With gentleness no fear is possible. Without fear and judgment, joy can enter your life. If you believe "God's will for you is joy", you can find acceptance and peace. The open hands of gentleness are always filled. The gentle have no pain. They cannot suffer. So, why wouldn't they be joyous? They're sure they are beloved, and they are safe.

As sure as grief goes with attack, joy goes with gentleness. God's teacher's trust in Him. God's voice directs them in all things. Joy is their song of thanks. In the Christian belief, it was through Christ's crucifixion that salvation was brought to many. Christ looks down on them in thanks. His need of them is just as great as theirs of Him. By sharing the purpose of salvation, there is joy. Out of great suffering came great joy. "I have told you this so that my joy may be in you and that joy may be complete." John 15:11NIV

By changing our perspective, we can be happy all the time. Yes, all the time! Asking God for help doesn't seem fruitful if He is capricious and sometimes punitive. Yet, if God is Love, He will guide us even when we can't predict a "joyful" result.

Sometimes people blame God for the shortages in their life saying it's not God's will for me. We need to replace such thoughts by saying, "I am a creature of god. God is abundant. I am a child of God. I came from abundance. God's will for me is abundance and joy."

Look To the Children

Looking to the innocence of little children helps me to see the world as it really is. I look at the way a child views a flower. They see the bright beauty and the petals and they laugh when you pull the petals off, one by one. They need to touch each petal before it falls to the ground; they laugh again when you feign surprise as they pluck off the next petal. It's so simple for them--something colorful, something to explore, and something to enjoy.

As Christ said, "We need to be as little children." Joy is found in simple things not in the complexities of life. There's a new spiritual place that we can come to if we're willing to give up ownership of the things of this world and see once again with the clarity of little children. We have to shed the adult role and humbly return to our true roles as God's children. A Paradox! A Divine Paradox!

So I can say with certainty that "God's will for me is joy!" I have come to understand that I may not always like what is happening to me in life, but if I accept life on life's terms, I'm joyful. Whenever I don't try to change a situation that can't be changed; whenever I don't hurt others, or myself; whenever I don't try to be right all the time; whenever I accept loss and return loved ones to God in good condition; then, I feel joy.

A Course In Miracles proposes that God, or Love, Itself, dwells within us because we were created in His image, making us extensions of His Love. If that is true, we are closest to our true nature when we're living in Love. Simply stated *A Course In Miracles* proposes the relinquishment of a thought system based on fear, and the acceptance of a thought system based on love.

6. DEFENSELENESS: The sixth characteristic of a spiritual teacher is defenselessness. Does what God created need defense? If we truly believe we're children of God, then we'll believe that "the strength of God in us is successful in all things." Therefore, we do not need defenses.

The idea of "defenselessness" is forcign in the everyday world that proclaims a theory of "the survival of the fittest". We defend our country when we are attacked and prepare to defend ourselves against all kinds of unforeseen threats. We do it in the name of "homeland security"--out of fear--and it makes sense. But the real power is not in things of this world, but in the world of the spiritual.

Eckhart Tolle in *A New Earth: Awakening to Your Life Purpose* says, " non-reaction is not a weakness but a strength. Another word for non-reaction is forgiveness. To forgive is to overlook, or rather to look through. You look through the ego to the sanity in every human being as his or her essence." Some Christian mystics called the "essence"--the Christ within; Buddhists call it your Buddha nature; for Hindus, it is Atman, the dwelling God. When we can look through a person to find that essence we can forgive.

In *A **Long Walk To Freedom***, Nelson Mandela wrote:"To make peace with an enemy one must work with that enemy, and that enemy becomes one's partner." He believed we are all partners with each other as children of God. By working with the white South Africans after his release from prison, Mandela became the leader of all of South Africa.

When we're in touch with our essence, our natural state, all our actions and relationships will reflect the oneness with all life that we can sense deep within. That partnership is universal Love. Mandela assumed that position of defenselessness and won over his previous enemies.

Spiritual realization comes when we see clearly that what we perceive, experience, think or feel is not ultimately who we are. We realize we cannot find ourselves in all those things that continuously pass away. We have a spiritual permanence, a formlessness, that Jesus called eternal life. We don't need to defend what is eternal as it needs no defense. As it says in Proverbs 68:31 NIV, "If God be for us, who can be against us?"

A teacher of God knows that once you look past illusions, nothing is there. The teacher of God learns this lesson slowly at first and then faster as trust increases. Mandela, a great spiritual teacher, proved that danger dissipates when defenses are laid down. Defenselessness is safety. It's peace. It's joy. It's God.

7. GENEROSITY: The seventh characteristic of a spiritual teacher is generosity. The term generosity has special meaning to the teacher of God. It's not the usual meaning of the word. In fact the meaning must be learned and learned very carefully. Like all other attributes this one rests on trust for without trust no can be generous in the true sense. To the world "giving away" means "giving up." To the teachers of God, it means giving away in order to keep. It's the exact opposite of the world's thinking.

The teacher of God is generous out of self--interest. But this reference to self is not the self of which the world speaks. The teacher of God doesn't want anything they cannot give away because he realizes it would be valueless to him by definition. What would he want it for? He could only lose because of it. The things of the world guarantee loss and bring suffering. What he does want to keep for himself are all the things of God. The things that are made for him as a child of God. These are the eternal things that he can give away in real generosity--even while he protects them forever for himself.

Since we are children of God, our primary relationship is between ourselves and God. We nurture our relationship with God by making conscious contact with Him. We contact Him by reaching within, by directing our minds to that loving place of comfort, by thinking and speaking of God.

The first thing we give to God is the acknowledgement of His place as a primary force in our lives. We reach out through prayer, reading and meditation. Meditation is primarily experiential; it is being still and knowing God. When we make contact with God, our spirits are charged and we have energy for other relationships.

The second step of giving comes when we are empowered by God; now, we're able to share that love with others. We cannot keep for ourselves the love we receive, we must give it away. When we are in close relationship with God, we become messengers of His love, of His Word. We show we understand God's message of Love by giving it away.

For some of us, this is a new concept! The idea that whenever we do something loving, it comes back to us. So giving and receiving are one. Real giving has little to do with the material world. Real giving means forgiveness, and Love.

8. PATIENCE: The eighth characteristic of a spiritual teacher is patience. When we're certain of the outcome of anything, we can afford to wait without anxiety. Patience is a natural attribute to a teacher of God. The timing of things does not bother the teacher of God because everything is in the "right time." The time will be as right as the answer is!

Sometimes people get caught up in a very dangerous pattern of rehashing the past. We say "What if" this had not happened or that had happened. The truth is the past served the person to which it happened. Perhaps it was not understood at the time or may still not be understood. Perhaps there are things that only God understands.

A teacher of God has patience with the past as well as the present, by becoming willing to accept all past decisions especially those that caused us pain. Out of all pain comes all learning. There are some benefits that can only be seen in retrospect.

When I left my second husband, I hit an all-time low. No one wants to leave a second marriage--it's usually makes you a two-time loser in the eyes of the world. Because he was consumed with sexual addiction, I was forced to leave him and the church congregation where he was a senior pastor. One week after the divorce, he remarried his first wife in that church.

Spirituality: A Life Force

Because I choose to remain silent, he kept his job and insinuated that our marriage just hadn't worked out and that he had made a mistake by divorcing his first wife. It worked for a few months until an irate husband of another woman took him before his Board of Directors.

I rehashed the past. My mind kept asking, "What if I had done this or that?" Even though the marriage was a horrific mistake crippled by his sexual addiction and my co-addiction, I wondered if I could have been done things differently. Should I have reported him? In time, I realized that I didn't need to ever second guess myself again because this marriage was a clear example of a relationship that was destructive to me and my spiritual well-being.

In later years, I realized that after the inevitable loss of that relationship, my spirituality bloomed. I discovered forgiveness through my study of *A Course In Miracles* in a new church. I wrote a new book about sexual addiction which today, 30 year later, still reaches readers every year. In my new church, I made friends, studied the Bible, and generally thrived. Co-addiction/codependency became an issue to work on to improve future relationships.

Because I had the patience to move forward from this terrible experience, I found a truly spiritual man who has been beside me for 25 years. Now I know I could never have come to this "holy relationship" without those difficult years. Because I trusted God and maintained a patient stance; that doomed marriage became a stepping stone to a better place.

Patience is natural to those who trust God. There's always that defining moment when we can say, "What is the lesson here? What does all this mean? Exactly, what am I being taught?" The teacher and the learner are inextricably joined in the learning process even when the lesson is not clear. Trusting the outcome of that process takes patience. I learned that for "everything there is a season, and a time to every matter under heaven--a time to weep, and a time to laugh: a time to mourn, and a time to dance...." (Ecclesiastes 3:1 RSV)

9. FAITHFULNESS: The ninth characteristic of a spiritual teacher is faithfulness. A teacher of God learns to replace fear with faith. Whenever they sense fear within themselves, they go back to God. A lack of faith could indicate we're impatient with some outcome, one we can't understand. Perhaps we're fearful of the future, or death itself. A teacher of God trusts with faith.

"Faith drives out fear" This concept helps me live my life. Every time I go back to old fears, I try to remember that I have an antidote to fear. If I go back to God, to the places I find God--to church, to prayer, to meditation--my fear will dissipate.

Sometimes I hang onto a problem, forgetting that God can handle any problem. All I have to do is turn it over to Him! Faithfulness requires that we give up everything, in faith, to our God. Therefore, there's no need for worry and fear. Reaching this level of faithfulness is a lifelong endeavor. The extent of the teacher of God's faithfulness is the measure of his advancement. Faithfulness is the spiritual teacher's trust in the word of God--to set all things right, not some, but all. As it says in Proverbs 28:20: "A faithful man will be richly blessed."

Years ago, I met a man who showed me this level of faithfulness. When the starving children were dying in Biafra, I met and worked with Father McHugh, a priest who had just come out of that civil strife. He came out under fire to tell the world of the plight of the children. We scheduled meetings with wealthy business men, asking them to send food--he spoke on radio shows, and TV programs. He spoke of how the children would line up in the food line; how many would drop dead as the line progressed; how some never reached the bowl of gruel held out by the priests. He was totally honest about how his heart ached to see this suffering; and how he suffered from the frustration of not being able to save them.

Father McHugh had a sense of mission, an urgency that was visible and contagious. When he visited our house, he would only eat one egg for breakfast. He wore no overcoat in the freezing weather because to buy one would take food from the children–we found one in the closet. There was no deterring him from his mission. We raised over 100,000 dollars for grain that would go back to Biafra with him. The morning he left, we were afraid to send him back under enemy fire but his faith directed him. This priest didn't seem to fear for his own life. He could've chosen to stay but he went back. That was faithfulness. He was a living example of Proverbs 5:3 NIV "Let love and faithfulness never leave you;…and write them on the tablet of your heart."

A Course In Miracles tells us that true faithfulness is consistent: "True faithfulness does not deviate. Being consistent, it's wholly honest. Being unswerving, it's full of trust. Being based on fearlessness, it's gentle. Being centered, it's joyous. And being confident, it's tolerant. Faithfulness confines within it, the other attributes of God's teachers."ACIM

10. OPEN-MINDEDNESS: The final characteristic of a spiritual teacher is open-mindedness. In Wayne Dyer's,10 Secrets for Success and Inner Peace, he claims open--mindedness to be the first secret. He goes on to say that having an open mind simply means being open to miracles--to the spiritual--to change. Open-mindedness seems easy until we recognize how conditioned we are by our past. Many current thoughts are influenced by the beliefs of our parents, our ethnicity, our gender, and the environmental influence of past experience.

True, most of our conditioning has come from well--intentioned cultural and societal forces but there are an infinite number of potentialities that have not been explored–we're simply not open to them. Usually, for most of us, "fitting in" superseded having a mind open to new ideas.

Wayne Dyer says the first step in opening your thought process is to refuse to allow pessimism into your consciousness. We need more minds that are open to anything and attached to nothing. Remember the universe with its billions of planets, objects and stars in our galaxy alone--and the uncountable galaxies out there. We know too little to be a pessimist. There are so many possibilities, miracles, mysteries. We can't afford to be narrow-minded about things."

A spirit of open-mindedness is the forerunner to change because it allows progress, growth, and creativity to flourish. The ability to participate in miracles--true miracles in our life--happens when we open our minds to our own limitless potential.

Dyer explains that our attachments can be the source of our problems. Some attachments include: the need to be right, the need to possess someone or something, the need to win at any cost, and the need to be viewed as superior. He claims these attachments hold us back from a spiritual life of peace and joy--from developing the characteristics of a spiritual teacher.

Spirituality: A Life Force

Wayne Dyer also says, "As a spiritual being, you can observe your body and be a compassionate witness to your existence. Your spiritual aspects see the folly of attachments because your spiritual self is an infinite soul. Nothing outside of you can really make you happy or successful. There are inner constructs inside of you that you bring to your world, rather than what you receive from it." Whenever I start thinking that someone or something outside of myself makes me unhappy, I have to go inside to check my thinking and realize that I'm the only one who can make me unhappy.

Sometimes open-mindedness simply means being willing to open you mind by observing and questioning the source of your own thinking. I have found that the more developed my spiritual identity, the more developed is my ability to question the thinking of my ego--my worldly self.

In *A New Earth: Awakening to Your Life Purpose*, Eckhart Tolle says," **The ego identifies with having, but its satisfaction in having is a relatively shallow and short lived one. Concealed within it remains a deep seated sense of dissatisfaction, of incompleteness, of 'not enough'. 'I don't have enough yet' by which the ego really means 'I am not enough yet.'"**

He goes on to explain there are many accounts of people who experienced joy--a new dimension of consciousness as a result of a tragic loss. Perhaps a loss of possessions in a disaster--loss of children to a tragic accident--loss of spouse or social position or reputation when a marriage ends--or the loss of physical attributes as we age. Eckhart explains that once the initial anguish and intense fear is experienced, it sometimes gives way to a sacred sense of Presence, a deep peace and serenity, that ushers in a complete freedom from fear. It brings us to a spiritual place of joyfulness, of peace.

In the next chapter, I will discuss the importance of making the shift from identifying oneself in a physical sense, with the body and our possessions, to open-mindedly viewing our spiritual identity as a child of God.

Chapter 3

A Spiritual Identity

Sometimes it takes an identity crisis to pull us into line spiritually. That's what happened to me. At one point in my life, I entered a second marriage and moved to another state. My new husband, an ordained minister, was called to another parish. So, I left my teaching job of twenty-two years, my retirement security, and my family and friends in the hopes of starting a new life.

In this move I was faced with a new city, a new state, and no job. After twenty-two years of teaching high school seniors, I found myself stripped of my identity. My own children were pretty well grown and taking care of themselves now so my job was to answer the phone at the parsonage and present myself as the minister's wife at church.

As I went to the unemployment office to collect my check, I felt disconnected, depersonalized and depressed. Longing for the fulfillment of human contact with my students, I grieved the loss of that role. No longer would I be greeted on the street by former students; no more would I see former students at the check-out at the supermarket. No one knew me! I felt like I had lost my identity!

I learned to be grateful for any human communication-- the gas attendant at the pump, the lady standing in line with me at the unemployment office, the man from the church who came to fix the dishwasher. But I still felt empty inside.

Then, I found out my husband was unfaithful and had been unfaithful several times in our time together--ultimately, the marriage fell apart. There had been signs of sexual addiction before the marriage but I choose to ignore these signals.

Right before we were married, I found several recent love letters written by women within the parish, and previous parishes. I was hurt to the core, but I forgave him and dismissed this symbolic "flashing red light" because I thought things would be different when we were married. After marriage, when a blatant affair was revealed, I realized I had given up everything that was a part of me for a marriage that was destined for divorce.

God, did I hurt inside! I hurt inside so much that I finally looked inside to my real self–my spiritual self. God was my only companion in those difficult days. It took a full year for me to recreate myself in the world--to find a teaching job, a place to live, to begin again. But, in that year of pain, I realized the most important lesson of my life. I am not an English teacher, I am not a wife, but I am God's child first!

The only "self" that sustained me through that terrible experience was my spiritual self. It remained ever strong, constant, and unchanging. I had found my true self by losing my worldly identity. Ironically, at this time I turned to another parish and was introduced to *A Course in Miracles*. Every week, I attended church services, bible study and group meetings which read *A Course In Miracles*. I met new friends and grew in my spiritual knowledge.

Spirituality: A Life Force

In time, I re--established my professional life as a teacher and began a new life as a writer. Ironically, on the day I was moving out of the parsonage, I received my first full-length book contract. Eventually, I met and married a truly spiritual man who is with me today--twenty-five years later.

Now, I can see what I gained spiritually from what seemed so difficult at that time. If I had not changed the emphasis of my identity, I would never be ready for the "holy relationship" I have today. Slowly, I began to incorporate those lessons in the books I was writing.

In one of my first books, entitled **Living In Love,** I was greatly influenced by this quotation from *A Course In Miracles*, "Your spiritual identity is that you are a child of God. We come from Love, Itself and live in God's Love." And influenced by this biblical quote, "You are from God and have overcome them, because the one in you is greater than the one who is in the world." John 4:4 NIV

Claiming A Spiritual Identity

After being influenced by these readings, I began to become more aware of my inner self. I began to question who I am and what is my role in everyday life. How do I view myself? Exactly, who am I? Why do I find it difficult to assume a spiritual identity? Is it because I think I am not enough?

Then, I realized I had attached my identity to the world– to my husband, to the church, to my profession--and these things were transitory things. No matter how much I achieved, attained, or possessed, it was never enough. The most important questions for me became "Who Am I?" And--"Why did I think I was not enough?'"

Question #1 Who Am I?

Who Am I? was my first question. I was so accustomed to identifying myself with what I had, what I accomplished, earned or what others thought of me, I'd lost touch with my original self. The innocent little girl that I was in my childhood.

Wayne W. Dyer, in his book, ***Inspiration: Your Ultimate Calling*** says: "The answer to this question is: I'm a unique portion of the essence of God. I originated in-Spirit, yet I've forgotten this fundamental truth. With this kind of awareness, we'd all be determined to seek our ultimate calling and live an inspired life."

When we see ourselves as children of God, our perception of ourselves changes, we are a spiritual being who's free of limitations and we trust that Divine Guidance is available at every moment. Some might hesitate to say, "I am of God", because it seems pompous and egotistical; however, the exact opposite is true. It's our ego, our own separated physical self that limits us to a non-spiritual identity.

Most people would agree that this is a purposeful Universe, with an intelligence supporting its creation and continuing evolution--and we're pieces of that intelligence by having emerged from it. It is my belief that "nothing comes from nothing". We have a divine origin; we are the product of the Universe, just as all manner of life is part of the whole. We came

Spirituality: A Life Force

here with a purpose--a divine purpose just as the leaves on the trees serve a purpose, just as the water in the stream serves a purpose. We are here--as a part of a Divine Plan--as children of God.

Dr. Dyer uses this analogy, "This is clearly a purposeful Universe, with an intelligence supporting its creation and continuing evolution--and we're pieces of that intelligence by virtue of having emerged from it. Consider, for example, that scientific analysis of even a droplet of blood reveals all the characteristics in our entire body's supply. The percentage of iron in that droplet is proportionately the same as in that which flows through our entire body--so it's easy to agree that the drop of blood is identical to the source from which it is removed."

Dyer further explains, "Now think what happens to that droplet when it remains in a state of separation: It can't fortify or heal us, and it will simply dry up, decay and disintegrate even though it contains all the physical properties necessary to survive that its original source does."

So when connected to our spiritual identity we function with purpose--as part of God, we are never removed from our Divine Purpose--our Source of life, of Love. There's no way to get in touch with your spiritual identity without this "spiritual awakening." When we become aware of who we really are, we can move from feeling like we're not enough--flawed, limited, imperfect--to completely comfortable with our own magnificence.

One of my journal entries right after my divorce, more clearly details my spiritual awakening: **"I've become aware of the power of God within me. It is a growing consciousness, and I need to keep in contact with that** power. His power can put me above selfish pettiness; it can move me in directions I would not dare move otherwise.

His power can sustain me through the pain of any loss. I've come to believe that the most important ingredient in my life is the power of God within. It will be my sustaining force until I return to Him. Those who love me will not sustain me, nor will the material possessions that make me comfortable, make me whole. Only that power of love within me that I call God can sustain me without fail.

Through the years, I've tried to experience my own sense of power in other persons, in position, and in things--and that would sustain me for a while. Eventually, though, that connection would dim. I then returned, again and again, to the spirit within where I found the power of God. That power never dims!

Today, when I am troubled or fearful, I think of this power of God within me, and I know I am loved. If I try to protect myself from all harm, I will be ineffective. But if I let God protect and guide me, I know I'll be cared for. God is a safe new place!"

Question #2 Why Did I think I was Not Enough?

In his book, **How to Raise Your Self-Esteem**, Dr. Nathaniel Brandon says that "how we feel about ourselves crucially affects virtually every aspect of our existence...as our responses to events are shaped by who and what we think we are". Dr. Brandon continues to say "that the tragedy is that so many people look for self-confidence and self-respect everywhere except within themselves and so they fail in their search." He goes on to describe positive self-esteem as a kind of "spiritual attainment".

Thinking you are not enough usually is a spiritual issue! It was for me. I disavowed the existence of the "Spiritual Self" and relied on my human powers alone, not the power and presence of God. My thinking I wasn't enough indicated my lack of faith and my misunderstanding of my true nature as child of God. For a period of time, I couldn't forgive myself for having made such a mistake in marrying such a sick man. I took on the sinful place of shame. In reality, it was simply an error in human judgment.

One of the reasons for not accepting our spiritual self is a lack of forgiveness. In our human frailty, we all sin. Yet, if we can't get beyond our sins, we may never see our spiritual selves--that is, the forgiven child of God. Self-esteem is the reputation we acquire with ourselves. When we remember only our mistakes, see only our frailties, and picture ourselves as sinful; we can't find that child of God within.

It's in our internalized conviction as children of God that we finally see that we are enough; in fact we are holy, chosen ones. It's in our connection with God, with Love, Itself that we learn to love ourselves, and live in the power and glory of God's Love. It's true that we are never enough in a human sense: but in the light of our inheritance as God's children and in the light of God's Love, we are everything, we are whole, we are perfect and we are enough! When I was going through my darkest period, a shameful divorce and complete public defeat, I had to let God into my life. Then, I became willing to change and was transformed not by magic but by process.

This spiritual transformation was a four step process!

For me, coming to believe that I am a child of God was the most important transformation of my life. It meant a re-imaging of self by first recognizing the child within. It was an internal re-imaging of self. I had to recognize and get in touch with that child that still lived within me by reaching back into my childhood and recognizing the hurt that happened to that child. Then I learned to nurture that child to correct "old tapes"--all the childlike feelings I held onto. Finally it became a matter of faith--based on God's promise of unconditional love and care. A change in self-esteem quickly followed which changed my whole world and my behavior. Here are the steps of my transformation:

Step 1: Recognizing the Child Within

For me, it meant returning to childhood, getting in touch with my inner child, and re-imaging that child into God's child. The first thing I did was to search for a picture of myself as a child. When I found it and positioned it on the shelf, I realized that if God was with me then and He was--then most certainly, God is with me now. I am still the same person. What a healing realization! Truly I was not a child of this world, not solely of my parents but a child of God!

Spirituality: A Life Force

This single experience enabled me to begin to get in touch with my inner child, to reach back and remember her as she really was. It was at that point that I started letting God in to heal her within me. My task became attending that child's needs, changing the negative messages given to her, and re-imaging that child into God's child.

Step 2: Acknowledging The Neglect that Child Has Known

The transformation began when I first acknowledged, without parental blame, the neglect that child had known. I needed to reach back to times when I felt unloved, to the dynamics of sibling rivalries, to the reality of parents who might have been unavailable. Had those experiences left that child lacking?

In a therapeutic setting, I was able to revisit my early years. Understanding that my parents did the best they could but were not perfect, I sought out places where I had been exposed to unhealthy influences like alcoholism. Earlier in my first book, **Claiming Your Own Life**, which covered adult children of alcoholics issues in general, I had explored the influence of alcoholism in my family. Now all this information came together! Now was the time to understand from a mature perspective that I could assure that child, assuage her fears and fill in the blanks from a childhood that may have been lacking.

Step 3: Nurturing that Child within

Third, I nurtured that child; and, finally, changed my perspective. I was able to counter any feelings of inferiority that lingered from youth. Ultimately, knowing in reality, I am in God, and with God--God's Child. There were times I was led back to an image of myself as "less than". I returned to seeking perfection, needing love while feeling unlovable, seeking control while feeling out of control, and looking for security in an unsafe world. All the childlike feelings I had known.

That was the time I needed to remind myself that I am perfect, and I am lovable, and I am safe and secure. Often, I simply said to myself, "I am a child of God." I came to believe that truth.

Step 4: Coming to Believe You Are A Child Of God.

The transformation became a matter of the faith perspective--the coming to believe. God did not make us to abandon us. He did not intent us to view ourselves and our environment with distrust. He did not intend us to return to old patterns: to feeling the fearful feelings of childhood; to seeking acceptance because we fear we are not acceptable; to desiring maturity but remaining a child. God made us to be His Children and promised us His unconditional love and care. Because I came to believe, my life changed.

Once this conversion was made, my fears began to dissipate and the world became safer; I began to embrace discipline and live a better life; I saw the human fallacy of perfectionism; and came to love myself as a child of God. Then, I expected to be respected and loved in return. Holy relationships became possible. I became grateful for my new self, which brought this new life of peace and joy. When I did not understand the world, I turned my fears to God, my father, who has all the power and all the answers.

First, as a child of God my world was safer

Before my transformation to a new spiritual identity, I was afraid. Whenever I relied on my own human frailties, there was always fear. But when I realized that I'm a child of God, I knew I would be protected and safe. After all, God, who is all powerful, would not abandon his creation, His child.

Even though I continued to see tragedy and sickness around me, the world had become spiritually safe for me because God is my parent, my Protector. I learned to listen to my inner self to discern what might be dangerous. When I sensed danger, I looked to God for the courage to proceed. Bad things did not elude me, but my perspective had changed.

My first initiation with trust developed by trusting God and, then, it spilled over to relationships with others. Over and over again, I turned my life and will over to the care of God as I understand Him; and, over and over again, He did not fail me.

Second, as a child of God I lived a better life

Before my transformation to a new spiritual identity, I desired to be a mature, moral person but often resorted to childlike reasoning. Now, I held myself in greater esteem and acted accordingly. There's a saying that I've often used, "act your way into good thinking." In the past whenever I felt bad about my circumstances, I would blame others for my situation. Now, as a child of God, I had the power to use discipline in my life. I had the discipline to end bad, hurtful relationships, to speak up for myself and others when I saw disrespect or abuse, to pray, to choose to live in peace and joy and to remain forever grateful for God's love.

My standards for myself were raised with this new spiritual perspective. No longer did I desire to be a mature, moral person, I became one! I acted my way into good thinking. And as I became more lovable, I began to love this new mature spiritual person.

Third, as a child of God I stopped trying to be perfect

Previously, because I felt "less than", I tried harder. There was a drive for perfection in all areas of my life. Perfectionism told me that I could reach perfection if I tried harder. It told me I could responsibly put all things in my life in order. I was playing God by taking control of everything.

Ultimately, it became clear to me that it was only through my connection with God that I could be OK. When I understood that I am God's child, not God; then, I accepted my limitations and failings. Simply, I forgave myself for my human failings. Accepting our true selves creates a paradox by asking us to forgive ourselves our human frailties on the one hand, and to view ourselves as perfect spiritual beings on the other. Only when we see through this seeming contradiction can we come to love ourselves.

Fourth, as a child of God I came to love myself

When we can come to understand ourselves as perfect spiritual beings, or children of God, we are ready to love ourselves as God loves us. It would be hard to conceive of the energy of God as a conditional force--one which picks and chooses its subjects to love. Therefore, we're asked to forgive ourselves of our imperfections and love ourselves unconditionally. Not always easy--but ever so vital for peaceful, positive, and powerful living. For me, I found that I couldn't really love another person until I loved myself. It's often said that you can't give away what you don't have. True love came to me only when I knew Love within myself.

Fifth, as a child of God I expected to be treated lovingly

Other very important issues were brought to light with this new perspective. Now, I had the right to be treated in a loving way. It became my responsibility to maintain my self-love and discipline. No longer could I allow abuse in my life! No longer could I live without the dignity due a child of God. So, I set limits in relationships, and communicated my needs in a loving way. No longer did I fear abandonment; therefore, I refused to accept physical or psychological abuse. The fears and codependency, that originally allowed me to have married a man who abused women, disappeared. After the divorce, from that broken place of displacement, and despair, I was able to re-establish myself as a teacher, sell my first book, and buy my own home. Eventually, I met and married a man whom I could love as he loved me.

Sixth, as a child of God I found gratitude, peace and happiness

As long as I played God, trying to control the world, I couldn't find happiness. When I let go and brought my will in line with God's, I found gratitude and peace and happiness. Every day I needed to say "God is very good to me and I'm grateful." Then, I just look around and find the things I can be grateful for. I still start my day this way.

I look to myself! If I'm not in physical pain, I celebrate! I think of a time when my body was wracked with pain and thank God for this pain free day. If I am in pain, I wait for the moment it eases. If I am able to see the snow falling on the window, I celebrate! And if I ever come to a place where I cannot see it, I will imagine it. Today I will be fed and in a warm home. Today I will be able to tell someone I love them.

If you are grateful and see yourself as a child of God, you will find hope and joy. Once we have found hope and joy, we will teach it. It's inevitable; we always teach what we are.

Seventh, as a child of God, I accepted God's will for me is joy

All of us want to live joyfully! Contented with the world around us, without the petty complaints, happy within: these are our goals. We can see joy in others but how do we get it? Joy is not found in the accumulation of wealth: it is found in the acceptance of God's goodness to us, in a benevolent universe, and in our connection with Love, itself.

It would be inconceivable that a loving parent could want anything but joy for His children. So it must be with God. Some people believe in a punishing God one that arbitrarily hands down judgments to teach us lessons. That is not my understanding of God. For me, God is Love, itself and I am His child.

I believe the tragedies that we experience come from the wayward way of an arbitrary material world. Expecting to understand all worldly suffering can become overwhelming. Perhaps we were never meant to understand it but to see it as a by-product of the material world. So much of what we see in our everyday living is seen through the wrong perspective, our human perspective. Perhaps the only permanent world is within our spiritual selves: that part of us that makes us children of God. I can readily accept that!

I don't know why life includes so many tragic shifts and changes and have failed in trying to make sense of it. But in some strange way, the world seems to work in conjunction with me when I cooperate with it.

Eighth, as a child of God I could "Let Go and Let God"

By recognizing my primary relationship with God, I can let go of the things of this world and not expect to understand them. With God's help, I let go of an addiction, and an addictive relationship--knowing these things were not meant to bring me joy. Loss always includes some sadness, but the sadness is easier to bear when I don't resist the change, when "I Let go and Let God."

Many times I didn't know the results of a loss until long after it had occurred, but I knew that God would never abandon me and that, in time, I would see some good from a seemingly bad situation. After all, in my lifetime, I had survived the loss of a parent at 14 years old, the tragic accidental death of a brother, the death of my child, and a devastating betrayal in marriage--and found a new spiritual identity through that loss.

By letting go to God and believing that the outcome of all events will be joy, I have discovered that, through acceptance, joy naturally evolves. Now living makes sense! Because of this step by step process of spiritual transformation to a new spiritual identity, as a child of god, my world changed completely. The next chapter on spiritual living gives more definition to these changes.

Chapter 4

Spiritual Living

If you believe you're a child of God, you can see others as children of God, and you will approach the world in a more spiritual way. When you change your mind about who you are, you become a spiritual teacher--a teacher of God. Now your own learning becomes complete through your teaching. You might ask, "What kind of course does the teacher teach?

A Course In Miracles Says, "The form of the course varies greatly as do the teaching aides. However, the contents of the course never changes. Its central theme is "You are God's child. You are innocent. You are saved."

It's difficult to find examples of this kind of teaching on CNN where greed, war and revenge consume the news. However, one news story caught my attention a few years ago:

On March 13th, 2005, Brian Nichols went mad and shot three people in and around an Atlanta courtroom. One of those killed was Judge Rowland Barnes, a respected, venerated judge, another Julie Ann Brandeau, the court stenographer, who just happened to be working in court that day. Also killed was Hoyt Teasley, a deputy who tried to apprehend Nichols.

After eluding the police and murdering a federal agent named David Wilhelm, Brian Nichols made his way that night to the apartment of Ashley Smith in Duluth, an Atlanta suburb.

Ashley was a widowed mother with a five-year-old daughter. Her husband had been stabbed to death and died in her arms. When Nichols captured her at gunpoint, she did not resist him. Rather she told him that if he killed her, her daughter would be parentless. But even more importantly, her sense of calm took over and she talked to Nichols about God's Love and the purpose of life.

Ashley asked him why he had killed so many people and he said he "was a soldier". Somehow in his twisted reason, he felt compelled to kill. At first, Nichols tied her up and she feared for her life. But Ashley didn't show her fear, she treated him "as a brother in Christ". In a loving way, she suggested that he should turn himself in to the authorities and stop the killing. Ashley explained about her husband and how violence had taken him from her and her daughter. Ashley became Nichol's teacher because she extended God's Love to him when most people would have recoiled–she lived what she believed in her heart-- that God loves all of us--no matter what our transgressions.

There was no panic, no hatred in her eyes. Together they listened while CNN blasted the story nationwide, repeating every detail over and over again. His face, his crime! She got her bible and a spiritual book, **The Purpose Driven Life** by Reverend Rick Warren. She read to him about the purpose of everyone's life. Perhaps he might be meant to help the prisoners where he was going. She convinced him he had the power to stop the rampage.

Ashley helped him buy a little time by helping him dispose of the truck he had parked outside her apartment. She didn't drive away when she had a chance. She returned to the apartment with the man who was accused of rape and had just murdered four people. He said he just wanted a reprieve of a few

Spirituality: A Life Force

hours–a well cooked meal. She cooked him pancakes. They ate together. Then, she quietly asked if she might go see her daughter at 9AM. He allowed her to go without him. She sensed he knew it was all over. As soon as she got in the car, Ashley called the police.

Brian Nichols was ready when the police got there. He waved a white flag and came out of the apartment peacefully. Later that day on CNN, the newscasters carried this remarkable story. Ashley recounted her ordeal in a calm peaceful way. She used words that are rarely heard on CNN talking about the will of God, talking about how he said she was an "angel of God." Talking about being "brother and sister in Christ"; talking about how all he needed was "hope."

I was anxious to see how the news media would react to this story. On the Fox Channel, Hiraldo Rivera and his guests spewed out words of hate about Nichols, a cold-blooded murderer, an alleged rapist, the scum of the earth. They seemed lost for words about the remarkable peacefulness of Ashley Smith, but full of words of hatred for Nichols. They seemed stunned that Ashley was able to see past his killings and treat him as "a child of God."

When Ashley met Brian Nichols, she didn't recoil from him thinking he was beyond redemption--even after he had just killed four people. She listened, she shared, she taught. Because she believed in him, her lesson was heard. There's a master plan which includes specific contracts to be made by each teacher of God. There are no accidents in salvation. We will meet those who are there for us to have the potential for a "holy relationship."

As I said in the last chapter, there's one transforming message we all need to be aware of and that is "You are a child of God"--you are perfect--just the way you are! And the message we all need to pass on is: "God loves you the way you are and I love you the way you are!" Ashley Smith projected this message to Nichols and he heard it. Ashley put into practice Christ's biblical directive:"Let us love one another, for love comes from God. Everyone who loves has been born of God and knows God. Whoever does not love does not know God, because God is love." 1 John 4:38 NIV

THE TWO VOICES--ONE OF OUR EGO--ONE OF GOD

Gerald G. Jampolsky, a pioneer in presenting ***A Course In Miracles*** concepts, has been one of my teachers. In his work, ***Out of the Darkness Into the Light--A Journey of Inner Healing***, he clearly details his transformation after reading ***A Course In Miracles***. There was a time for Jampolsky when he realized that he had been listening to the voice of his ego--a voice of fear that told him he was "alone in a world of scarcity". He attempted to rely on his own intellect, will, judgment and past experience only to feel empty and isolated. For him, love was always conditional in those days.

Jampolsky says: "Through my study of ***A Course In Miracles***, I began to realize that there are only two ways to make decisions. The first one was already familiar to me; the old way of listening to the ego, the voice of fear and separation. The second was one I just began to learn, which was to listen to the voice of God, a voice based on love and joining."

My writing has always been a product of my own spiritual journey--lessons learned that begged for expression. My first

Spirituality: A Life Force

book, ***Claiming Your own Life As An Adult Child of an Alcoholic*** written in 1989 and reprinted in 2007, details my experience growing up with alcoholism and my spiritual journey into sobriety. The spiritual lessons continued and more books came. In 1993, I published a book called ***Living in Love: Connecting To The Power Of Love Within*** which marked my struggle to live-in-love, to come out of the darkness into the light of God's Love. Some of those ideas matured into this book about spirituality in general. In 1998, I published ***Holy Relationships*** with Morehouse Publishing, a religious press for the Episcopalian Church. A biblically based small gift book, it emphasizes the spiritual edge of intimacy and the importance of placing God at the center of any relationship. Chapters five and six of this book bring to light those ideas in more detail. It wasn't until I met and married my present husband, who is truly a spiritual man, that I really understood "holy relationship". We have been together for 25 amazing, happy years.

THE VOICE OF MY EGO

When I started writing about spiritual issues there were times my ego said: "No one will listen to this message. Who are you to pretend to have something to say about love, about God? Who do you think you are anyway? Why do you think you have a spiritual message? "

Sometimes, especially after I received a rejection slip or failed to achieve a goal, the voice got more negative and more persistent with these messages: Until I read in ***A Course In Miracles***, the voice of my ego told me: "You're unprotected.

You're unlovable. You're alone in a frightening world. Nothing can save you! You're not safe. There's no point in trusting anyone or anything because people, places, and things will harm you. Be careful--take care of yourself!"

My ego told me I'd better remember the past so I would not be hurt in the future. It made me hate failure and helped me make idols of people. It helped me to "people-please", be unforgiving, blame others, live as a victim, or look for an "exclusive love" to make me happy.

The voice of my ego told me that if I looked carefully, I could find one special love relationship that would bring me happiness. It told me to think of myself and my family first, and get as many material things as I could. It told me to demand and get my way, to manipulate people and control others. It helped me measure people by what they had and what they could do for me. The voice of the ego had lead me astray!

With this dialogue going on in my mind, it's no wonder I felt a sense of "impending doom." as if I was defeated before the battle had begun.

A NEW VOICE EMERGED

Finally, as I explained in Chapter Three, I came to accept my role as a child of God and accept and love others as His children as well. With this oneness came peace; with this oneness came courage and hope.

In Hugh Prather's work, ***There is a Place Where You Are Not Alone, Reflections on A Course In Miracles,*** he says: "What we know we know because we are one. In our oneness is perfect knowledge and peace, but in our conflict, controversy and specialness, there can be only despair. Even though they may choose to hear it at different times, God speaks to His children all at once."

Believing that there was a scarcity of love only made me conserve it. There could never be enough! Believing that defensive attack thoughts could protect me, I set up barriers, looking for a security I didn't need. In truth, I was terrified of my own impending doom, ultimately my death, and my final separation. It seems the very autonomy I sought was destroying me. Finally, I was forced to give up--to surrender!

Marianne Williamson in ***A Return To Love***, says: "Surrender is not weakness or loss. It is a powerful nonresistance. Through openness and receptivity on the part of the human consciousness, spirit is allowed to infuse our lives, to give meaning and direction."

Ashley Smith gave the world a clear example of the love of God in her treatment of Brian Nichols but the news story was soon dropped because it seemed it wasn't interesting enough--or was it that few could understand its great significance? I believe it was the most significant story of the year. Finally, in 2008, Brian Nichols was sentenced to life in prison where he remains today. When Ashley was called to testify against him, she did in a non-threatening way.

THE VOICE OF GOD SPEAKS IN DIFFERENT TERMS

For years, I looked for my identity in the diversion of codependent relationships, the temporary escape of alcohol, and in the gathering of material possessions. The relationships were transient, the alcohol lead to disease and despair, and the material possessions were never enough.

It took surrender for me to find peace, joy and even glory. I had to lose in order to win. When I established my true identity in my spiritual self, I understood my real purpose in life. When I recognized I come from God--the source of Love itself, I could distinguish between the voice of my ego, and the voice of Love, itself. Then I came to know we all have the same message of love in us and we all need to hear it and express it. For that reason, I can say I love you because we are one.

A CHILD OF GOD CHANGES BEHAVIORS.

Once I had internalized the concept of being a child of God, I could change old behaviors. Now I could ask those important questions! Is this decision the loving one? Is this action self-destructive, self-effacing or self- indulgent? A child of God lives differently from a child of the material world; yet, we all live in and of this world.

In his books, Dr. Jampolsky tells the wonderful story of how he made the loving decision to treat his patients without charging fees. It was a daring move! Then, when his first book, **Love Is Letting Go of Fear**, became a runaway best seller, his financial problems were solved.

We may not all make such drastic changes in our living circumstances as Jampolsky did but we can experience change through surrender and learn to hear the voice of God. Marianne Williamson, in *A Return To Love*, says:"Something amazing happens when we surrender and just love. We melt into another world, a realm of power already within us. The world changes when we change. The world softens when we soften. The world loves when we choose to love the world.

What was striking about Ashley Smith's story was that she was able, even as she feared for her life, to show Nichols love,–to validate his worth--knowing he had recently killed several people. Ashley explained that she too had sinned and had lived through many hardships but she had surrendered to God. She became his teacher!

A CHILD OF GOD CAN'T ALLOW THEMSELVES TO BE MISTREATED.

Ever? No never! When disrespect happens, I will note it and confront the situation, if appropriate; and THEN quietly, lovingly go on with the confidence that the person trying to harm me is not aware of their own loving nature. I am who I am, a loving child of God, and that never changes. Their attempt to harm me is their "cry for love". I need only refuse to accept the abuse and respond lovingly. My peace of mind is still intact!

A CHILD OF GOD REJECTS SELF-ABUSE.

If I believe that I am of love, of God itself, I would not knowingly harm myself. How could I try to destroy one of

God's children? How could I devalue what God values? Therefore, I have to reject self abuse.

So it is that we find it difficult to love another until we love ourselves. Here are some simple rules for loving yourself:

1. **Be gentle with yourself--** Everything takes time. Therefore, give yourself the time you need to love yourself. When you forgive yourself, you lift a great weight off your shoulders. All of us are at exactly the place we need to be at any given moment. Give yourself permission to grow and to come to the awareness of life. What is your hurry? Be kind, but not indulgent. Be kind to yourself. You are God's child.

2. **Be kind to your mind--**Fill your mind with positive affirmations. You are worth it. Don't abuse your precious mind with negative thoughts and digressions. Say nice things to yourself every day. Begin with the words, "I am God's precious child." Be kind to your mind by praying, meditating, reading positive words and visualizing positive outcomes.

3. **Stop criticizing yourself--**Loving ourselves means that we don't beat ourselves up by telling ourselves that we are bad or dumb or

Spirituality: A Life Force

worthless. Stop mercilessly judging yourself. There is nothing wrong with you. You are God's child.

4. **Stop scaring yourself**--Sometimes we carry around a sense of impending doom. Let it go! You do not need to be afraid. Fears of abandonment and rejection are not real, so stop scaring yourself. There is nothing to fear when you rely on the love and power of God.

5. **Praise yourself**--Don't listen to your own negative defamations. Give them up in favor of positive affirmations of praise. Tell yourself, "I am wonderful." Not just once, but all the time. You are a wonderful child of God. Praise your strengths and accomplishments. If you can do it for even one minute at a time, it will help. Talk to yourself as a loving God would talk to His child.

6. **Accept all things as good and be grateful**--So often we see only the negative side in an event or happening. Look for the positive side. Ask yourself, "What is the lesson which I must learn?" Look for it and be grateful.

Whenever a self defeating thought comes to my mind, there needs to be a voice that says, "I am God's child". It's difficult to rationalize self-destructive behaviors like consuming mind altering drugs, or living co-dependently, when your mind is saying "I am a child of God.

"It's difficult to engage in any negative behaviors when your inner child says, "I love you, my God." and the answer comes, "I love you, too, my child." How much more nourishing are these words than the self-destructive messages of the ego!

A CHILD OF GOD EMBRACES A DISCIPLINED LIFE.

Today, I see discipline as the commanding force of love. Real love does not harm others, take from them, or leave them broken and afraid. So it is with living as a child of God! We start by cleaning our own house by clearing out the dishonesty, the intolerance and the lack of discipline in our lives. My disciplined life began thirty--seven years ago when I got sober and accepted a disciplined life guided by ethical values.

First, I had to admit I was powerless over alcohol. Seek help from God and turn my life and will over to the care of God. Then I had to make a fearless, searching moral inventory asking God to remove my defects of character. Then, I made amends for wrongdoing and began taking a personal inventory every day. Finally, through this disciplined life brought more prayer and meditation and ultimately a spiritual awakening.

A CHILD OF GOD CONTACTS GOD THROUGH PRAYER.

Spirituality: A Life Force

When we seek God, we are actively searching. Unlike some common misconceptions, prayer is not a passive endeavor. I associate peacefulness with prayer because praying may bring peace of mind--but, the act of praying itself implies a conscious effort on our part to contact God. Therefore, in order to have a prayer life, I need to develop a program of prayer. Having a regular program of prayer implies times of prayer and meditation as a normal part of everyday life. Even though there are many prescribed ways to pray or meditate, we are free to seek our own ways. I believe I need to seek contact with God each day.

Somehow, I couldn't really accept prayer into my life until I began to reap the benefits of it. Practicing a program of prayer made me feel better, think better, and live better. That's a difficult combination to turn away from. Once I set my program for prayer in motion, it began to carry me.

Somehow when I start my day right, it stays right. As a recovering alcoholic with thirty-nine years of sobriety, I always start my day with a simple request that God might keep me away from one drink for one day. Then, I go on to the daily meditation book of my choice. I've used different books over the years because I have changed in my spiritual growth. There are many ways to choose to start the day.

No matter what the day brings there's an unending source of power for us to draw on through prayer. All we need do is to connect and reconnect with God's power throughout the day. During the day I remind myself with these prayerful phrases:"God is with me. I live and move in Him." "Peace to my mind. Let all thoughts be still." "This is the day I choose to spend in perfect peace." "God is the Love in which I live." (Course In Miracles p 430,392,412)

Ending the day in prayer has special meaning. It can be a time of inventory when we ask God to help us see what might have gone wrong during the day. It can be the moment we ask for forgiveness and resolve to make amends; and, the moment we thank God for another day.

Evening prayer doesn't necessarily need to be structured as you kneel beside your bed. It can just be a heart to heart talk with God before you sleep. Prayer is a wonderful way to end a day! By lifting my heart to God in daily prayer, hope, peace, and joy are restored to me. That is my daily grace, my personal miracle.

A CHILD OF GOD PUTS GOD FIRST.

Living as a child of God implies a workable relationship with God with communication and involvement. In all relationships, I expend certain energies to be successful. So it is with God. That is not to say God ever abandons us or withholds love from us, but if we are to reap the amazing benefits of a personal relationship with God, we need to place our relationship with God before all other human relationships.

But what about my wife, husband or children? How can anyone come before them? God is our primary source of Love, of peace, power and glory. Through our spiritual connection with God we reach out to the spirit of those we love. It is really all one Love, but so often we forget, "God is the Love in which we live."

Spirituality: A Life Force

Recently, I heard a member of my church group say that he had always felt a certain "spiritual disquietude" that could only be filled with his relationship with the Divine. For him, nothing else could fill the emptiness inside. I knew exactly what he meant!

My feeling of emptiness didn't mean that God ever left me but I choose to move away from God. Other relationships became primary--my husband, my children, other family members. I lost track of the fact that "God is the Love in which I live." First and foremost, it is God and me. All other relationships fall into place when I recognize this truth. If I am to bring strength and courage and hope to anyone else--where will I get it? By making contact with God, and by relating to others in a loving way.

At times, making a human relationship primary and neglecting God has caused me to lose my way. When I find myself co--dependently relying too much on a spouse or child for inner meaning, I feel a spiritual void. Then, I re-evaluate my relationship priorities, restructure my relationships, and give more time to God. The peace and joy return.

When anything is important to you, you devote yourself to it. Your primary relationship with God is the most essential thing in your life. Yet, if you don't attend to it, you won't reap the benefits of the union. The inner spiritual void will remain!

People often say they need more time to work around the house, to relax, to play, or to be with friends or family. How often do people say they need time to pray or get re-connected with God? A spiritual relationship is personal and requires reflective, quiet times. It doesn't just happen since it's an intentional pursuit!

Christine A. Adams

A CHILD OF GOD NEEDS TO BE ALONE WITH GOD

Sometimes when I need to get back to God, I go back to Maine where I was born. Across from the house where I grew up, there's a suspension bridge that spans a portion of the York River as it makes its way out to sea. The river feeds into the harbor here and sometimes it holds more beauty than I can bear. I went there when my father died, then, my brother, my mother, my child, and my first husband. Each time the flow of the water energizes my soul, and the beauty of the sunset brings peace.

Other times I go to the ocean in Maine, where I find a flat rock high above the other rocks and sit in the sun. It's the calm of the rock that is so familiar, the gray white slate colors that dry as the day goes on. Barnacles, snails, and seaweed, ugly and beautiful at once lie at my feet while crabs crawl around the sea floor to keep me company. Paths by the ocean are overgrown with red and white sea roses to decorate my place; a quiet place of gentle beauty that reminds me of God's power and permanence. There, I am alone with God.

It's in these quiet places that I recognize my part in God's universe is simply to accept whatever changes come to me, to go on without holding onto the pattern of yesterday and to see what beauty is in this day. In these sacred places, I turn to God like a child, giving Him control of my life, letting Him guide me. Once again, I recognize my prayerful connection with God as my most important relationship. Once again, I feel loved, protected, and cared for at all times. In these places, I come home to Love, itself.

Spirituality: A Life Force

By paying too much attention to human relationships, career goals or even the care and management of a home, we can lose our spiritual center, fail to contact God, and forget that He is our primary relationship. When that happens, we are looking for happiness in the material world of other people and things. That never works! Real joy is inside of us.

Contact with lovers, friends, and family bring special joyous moments because we receive what we give. But first we need to give to God, we need to have our spirits charged. It takes energy to give of ourselves. When there's little energy inside, we are soon depleted.

When I become overwhelmed with the ups and downs of life, I feel powerless. Yet, when I am in the right place with God, there is always enough power not only to deal with the obstacles of life, but also to accept them. God, the creator of all love, gives me enough love to live, to forgive, to accept, and to grow. My first step must be to give of myself in this primary relationship with God. Then, I receive His Love and am ready to go on with my life!

A CHILD OF GOD SHARES THE LOVE OF GOD

Once we have given ourselves to this love relationship with God, the next thing we must do is to share that love with others. We cannot keep to ourselves what we receive from God. In order to keep it, we must give it away. In this sense, we become the messengers of God's Love, of His word. Ashley Smith demonstrated this when she was able to show love to Brian Nichols, to share how she had turned her life around through the love of God, and to change his mind about who he was and what his purpose in life might be.

A Course in Miracles says:"A messenger is not the one who writes the message he delivers. Nor does he question the right of him who does, nor ask why he has chosen the message he brings. It's enough that he accept it, give it to the ones for whom it is intended, and fulfill his role in its delivery."(ACIM WB 154)

When we are in close relationship with God, we become His messengers–exactly like Ashley Smith did. We perform our part by accepting His message of Love for ourselves; then we show we understand God's message of Love by giving it away. We choose no roles that are not given by Him and gain by every message of love we give away. Ashley Smith gained the rest of her life-- more years with her daughter, Paige. What an amazing spiritual teacher she was!

A CHILD OF GOD DISCERNS GOD'S MESSAGE

Once we have established a primary relationship with our Creator and accepted our place in the universe as His children, we are ready for our life's work. We turn our will and our life over to the care of God as we understand Him. As God's children, we already have all we need. We are complete in our own oneness with God. Therefore, it matters little what we do for a living. How we execute our chosen career does not matter in this work of loving others. It didn't matter to Brian Nichols that Ashley Smith was a waitress who had gone back to college to study to be a medical technician; it mattered that she showed him love and concern.

We're here to project God's message of Love, not to operate a tractor trailer truck, write a legal document, pave a road, cure a patient, or lecture to an audience. We are of love, Itself, of God and our purpose is to love. We can bless the world when we use the surgeon's knife, or teach someone the alphabet, serve someone a bowl of soup, or scrub the floor. We can love wherever we are!

All of us are messengers--we will project some message whether it be God's message of love, or messages of fear, resentment, and hatred. We will cry out for love, or we will give love, either way bringing a message to the world. It is our choice to teach love or fear.

By turning our life and will over to the care of God, we are making the decision to go with God's purpose, and God's purpose can only be a loving one. It's no coincidence that Ashley Smith was sharing Reverend Rick Warren's bestselling book, **The Purpose-Driven Life** with Brian Nichols. She explained to him that we all have a purpose in life and that he did too. Perhaps he would be needed by someone in prison--his life was not over.

It's not always necessary that we understand the direction of our lives, but it's essential that we trust in the purpose. Our purpose can only be to bless the world in God's Love. That is the essence of living a spiritual life.

A CHILD OF GOD SEES EVERYONE AS ONE--AS GOD'S CHILDREN

This realization removes pride, prejudice and judgment. In our spirit selves, there are no differences in us! Our purpose is to reach out in love to all that touch our lives. It doesn't have to be the sick and suffering children in Africa. It can be the weary senior citizen who bags the groceries at the supermarket. We can help him out by putting a few of the groceries into the bag, smiling and saying thank you. Let him know you love and appreciate his work.

A CHILD OF GOD CHANNELS GOD'S LOVE.

All we need do is recognize the opportunities for love that are ours. Living in the moment can mean giving a child who stutters time to speak, listening to a friend's concerns about her husband's health, being grateful to know that child or that friend. Through our loving attention, we can give others the gift of love. Even when we are in emotional pain, we can be grateful for the opportunity to feel our feelings and to grow to a new place of emotional strength. Even when we have been betrayed, we can be grateful for the opportunity to grow through forgiveness.

Speaking loving words to others is not that difficult. Through our loving words, we can provide the fodder for a positive inner voice within others. We can bring to their subconscious messages that may return to them when they have lost confidence, or are afraid. Words of love are powerful tools that shape future positive actions!

Spirituality: A Life Force

Once I refused to speak to someone who cared for me. We had come to the point of ending a relationship when he relapsed into addiction. I had asked him not to contact me again, but it was Christmas Eve so he called anyway. Out of fear I refused to enter into the conversation. I said I did not want to speak with him at this time. I was forceful, adamant, and explicit. Ten days later, he overdosed. I was denied the opportunity to ever speak to him again. Since that day, I try to speak what I feel, but respect and honor all loving acts of others.

Recently, it struck me that I owe a great debt to my daughter. She has always been emotionally available to me, patient with me, and most loving to me. We have an unusual relationship. Then, I realized how necessary it was that I speak those words to her. Just because something "is" doesn't mean that it's always recognized. I couldn't wait until the proper time to tell her what she means to me. It was a simple thing--we were together at a local restaurant having breakfast on a Saturday morning, as we have done so many times. I said "I want you to know how much I love you and value our relationship. I am blessed to have you in my life." She has since told me she thought of that moment many times.

Through acceptance of my role as a child of God, I can bring peace to others. It's emotionally destructive to seek anything but peace of mind; therefore, peace is my goal. Living in the moment means asking myself in all situations: "What is the loving thing to do in this situation?" "How can I restore peace to this scene?" "What is my part in this?" "How can I be a channel of God's love here?" When I find my inner answers to these questions, I am living--in--love.

Christine A. Adams

A CHILD OF GOD PRODUCES LOVE IN THE WORLD

It doesn't matter what our gifts may be, all gifts are of God. It was as a writer, that I first began to see my gifts "spring into my sight and leap into my hands". For a brief moment, I tried to claim these gifts because my ego told me they were mine. I began to plan trying to control my success. Almost immediately, I recognized the fallacy in that thinking. I decided to write what was in my heart and leave any worldly success to God. That took my ego out of the picture and let me speak directly to the reader.

A Course In Miracles reminded me to let go of what I claimed as mine. Now, I use my gifts to speak of God's Love but I don't claim these gifts. It's the Holy Spirit that leads the way in my writing and I follow. There's little difficulty with decision making in my choice of subject as I am lead from one awareness to another. The goal is to speak what I learn, to give it away to others--in love. There's no other goal!

In *A Return To Love*, Marianne Williamson says: "We make decisions by asking the Holy Spirit to decide for us. There are always so many factors in life that we can't know. We make no decisions by ourselves, but ask how we might be most helpful in carrying out His plan. The moral authority that this attribute gives creates a star like quality. It is our humility, our desire to be of service that makes us stars. Not our arrogance."

As I write with this purpose in mind, I find myself energized by the process. It's not an arduous task that drains me of all my energy. It's a process that brings me energy, helping me to hear my own lessons, letting me learn as I teach, allowing me to receive as I give to you.

Giving and receiving have become one in my writing. As I expend the energy to reach out to you, new energy comes forth revitalizing me. I never tire of the task for it has long ago ceased to be anything but a labor of love. So it should be in the use of any God-given gift, whether it is creative or commercial. It really doesn't matter what I do but it matters very much why I do it! I have to ask myself: "Am I teaching love in what I do? "Am I living as God's child each day?" One of my favorite quotes and the inspiration for this book comes from the main text of **A Course In Miracles: "Any situation must be to you a chance to teach others what they are, and what they are to you. No more than that, but also never less."**

Teaching God's Love in not only the work of writers, artists, priests and missionaries, it's the work of the corporate president, the waiter, the janitor, the lawyer and the unemployed. It doesn't matter what you do, it only matters how you live. There's no other choice except to live--in love if we are to be true to our spiritual selves. We do it by seeing all people as ONE, by gratefully living in the moment, and by using our own unique gifts to bless the world.

So far in this chapter I have only spoken of giving, not of receiving. The reason is giving and receiving are one. Whatever you give in love, in peace, and in healing will be yours.

But, still you might ask, "What do I receive?"The same things that you give! It is such a simple truth that sometimes the power of it eludes us. *A Course In Miracles* says: "You understand that you are healed when you give healing. You accept forgiveness as accomplished in yourself when you forgive. You recognize your brother as yourself, and thus do you perceive that you are whole." (ACIM WB 293)

By living in a loving way what do you receive? The greatest gift of all. Peace! ***The Course*** says: "Peace comes to those who choose to heal and not to judge." Whenever we make a conscious choice to forgive, to heal a situation, we are giving the gift of peace to ourselves as well as the other person. It's like a circle where the peace you give comes right back to you. Could there be a better gift?

A Course in Miracles maintains we are the essential instruments of peace for the world and that our thoughts and actions determine how widely it's shared. We become the means of peace when we are willing to learn, to teach, to give, and especially, to forgive.

There's an enormous difference between an unforgiving thought and forgiveness. An unforgiving thought is frantic in its intent, twisting relentlessly to pursue its goal. It holds distortion as its purpose, and in a furious attempt, it tries to smash the reality of anything that gets in its way--any contradictory point of view. Forgiveness, on the other hand, is still, and quietly does nothing. It doesn't twist things to fit its point of view, but merely looks, waits and judges not.

It seems ironic that by exerting no effort to judge, we can come to a peaceful place. It seems strange that by expecting nothing we can gain it all. If I must be right, or better or anything more than you, I will not be at peace. Peace of mind brings happiness to me! Peace of mind brings me spiritual joy. It brings me to a oneness with myself and a oneness with you. Then, there's no reason to be right or wrong, or more or less--that's not necessary with God's children.

Spirituality: A Life Force

What may seem unfair to me may cause me to lose my peace. But it's not my job to judge the fairness of life, to interpret the vagaries of the material world. It's my job to joyfully accept my true nature as a spiritual being, a child of God. Only then can I see you in the same light; only then will you respond to me in peace and love.

It's the function of love to unite not divide–to hold all things together. When we are loving, we attract love to us. It's as if the light of God's love that's within us draws the love of others to us. We become the messengers for God's love. In whatever we do, we teach love. We forgive! We heal! And, ultimately, it all comes back to us bringing us healing, love, and peace. The circle is complete, through God, through love, itself.

Chapter 5

Spiritual Relating

Spiritual relating happens in many learning-teaching situations. It seems that certain pupils have been assigned to each teacher--and show up at precisely the right moment. Why did Brian Nichols choose Ashley Smith's apartment building? Why did my students, Josh, and Sarah, come into my life when I needed them? Some relating seems to defy coincidence.

The Three Levels of Teaching

1. A Casual Encounter--he first level of teaching seems to be quite superficial. It consists of what seems to be a casual encounter: a chance meeting of two apparent strangers. But these chance meetings may be very meaningful because each has the potential of becoming a teaching-learning situation. Even if there's ever so brief a connection, it's possible for two people to lose sight of their separate interests and come together for a "holy instant."

We seem to learn as much as we need at the time. So, in that sense there are no differentiations between a chance encounter and a more developed relationship. One day in early recovery from alcoholism, I was particularly despondent and couldn't seem to find my way back to gratitude, to God. I decided to go to a church service but somehow peace and acceptance alluded me. I was afraid of my own dark place. I just wanted to hide in my own despair.

As I was leaving the church, I remembered that I had left my umbrella in the pew. So disgruntled and irritable, I trudged back into the vestibule. Just as I got inside, I noticed a young woman getting up from the last pew about to leave the church. Her face was totally covered with a fiery red purple birthmark. She looked down and hurried on by me. The image of her face never left me. She had every reason to want to hide but she didn't. That day, that girl was my teacher.

2. A Longer Relationship--The second level of teaching-learning situations can involve a longer more sustained relationship; in which, for a time two people enter into a fairly intense relationship and then appear to separate. It almost appears like some relationships end when each person has simply learned the most he or she can learn at that time.

I know in my life, I choose to leave my first marriage when I felt like the light in my soul was burning out. For me, to stay would have been akin to a spiritual death. The lesson was learned and I needed to move to a new spiritual place.

3. A lifelong Relationship--The third level of teaching-learning situations occurs in relationships that are lifelong. In these long term situations, the person is given a learning partner who presents her with unlimited opportunities for learning. These lifelong partners may not recognize their "holy relationships"; they may even seem to resist the idea; but if they decide to learn the lesson--the perfect lesson is before them and can be learned.

We may have such long term relationships with parents, siblings and other friends and family. Because these relationships change and grow with the transience of life, we grow and change through them. I have been privileged to have lifelong relationships with family members that continue to provide learning-teaching situations. The ultimate goal is always the same to make a relationship a holy one--one in which both partners see each other as one--that is, as innocent children of God.

In 1994 when I met Bob, my husband today, I knew we had a relationship that was different. There was never any question about us getting married. We were spiritually compatible and that made all the difference. We've been together 25 years and our relationship is as strong today as it was at the beginning. In my mind, there's no doubt that our relationship is a "holy relationship".

Soul Touching: Relationship As A Calling

Figuratively and literally, we're all on a spiritual journey. Initially, we hear a call to relationship. But if we have not faced our own demons and touched our own soul by establishing a connection with the Divine within us; if we have not recognized God's love for us, we will be unable to love another totally. Louise L. Hay writes in **The Power Is Within You**, "We usually make loving ourselves conditional, and then when we are involved in relationships, we make loving the other person conditional also." Conditional relationships often fail.

Christine A. Adams

As Thomas More states in **Soulmates,** "Intimacy begins at home, with oneself. It does no good to find intimacy with friends, lovers and family if you are starting out from alienation and division within yourself." For those who love themselves, the path of love is open. The first reward of self-love comes in the form of a new found sacredness in relationship.

Loving yourself has sometimes been misconstrued in our society. In this book, self-love has a spiritual meaning. Here, we are not talking of the narcissist whose love of self is so obviously self-serving. A person who views all others by what they can do for them--to enhance their own self image. How little self-love the narcissist has is demonstrated by how much he needs to fill the empty place inside! Speaking of Donald Trump, the noted scholar, Bill Moyers said that most people seem to have a "soul inside" but Donald Trump seems to have only an "open sore". I believe that Trump has demonstrated that he is never at peace with himself, or anyone else. That agitation to me may demonstrate "a terrible turmoil of spirit"--a lack of knowledge of the healing power of God's Love.

In Bill Moyer's studies of mythology, he often has spoken of how "a supreme ordeal" can bring a hero to a spiritual place. For me, that was true as I explain later in this chapter. For me, it was a devastating second marriage. When I had failed in this relationship, by my human frailty, I was brought to the only thing I had left--to God and my spiritual self.

When you touch your soul, you touch Love for that is what you are. This biblical verse makes it as clear as it can be. "Let us love one another, for love comes from God. Everyone who loves has been born of God and knows God. Whoever does not love does not know God. For God is Love." (1 John 4:7,8

NIV) When we love ourselves, we are "knowing" God; when we love another, we are also "knowing" God. Because God is Love. That is soul touching--the coming to know God--the coming to know love, the coming to know each other. Now comes the invitation to enter a "holy relationship" which is merely the touching of two souls. First, let us define the "unholy relationship" which pervades our society.

What Is An Unholy Relationship?

In an unholy relationship, there's a sense of being incomplete and a need to draw from the other. Deepak Chopra, in ***The Path to Love***, uses the term attachment to describe this unholy state. He explains that attachment to a lover makes people feel safe because they create a "we two" enclosed world. He further explains that this kind of attachment, or neediness, has a deeper spiritual meaning. It represents an attempt to reach unity by merging with another soul--not touching, but merging. Chopra claims that although it may not be completely conscious, at some level the partners realize that they have been living in separation from God. This separation is full of anxiety and insecurity, as each partner sees themselves as fragmented from the whole and in need of completeness.

An unholy relationship is based on deficiencies of Self; a holy relationship is based on spiritual completeness. If you have come together to be completed; if it is sex, money, status or approval that you are looking for in a partner, you are looking to use someone to complete you.

The truth is you are enough within yourself. It's enough to know you are born of God, connected to God, and that you are Love, itself. Once you have surrendered to this spiritual concept, you can accept the invitation to enter a holy relationship.

Examples of unholy relationships are broadcast on TV every day. Talk show hosts, like Dr. Phil, are eager to use them as examples. Recently, I watched Dr. Phil talking to a young woman about a man who had been physically abusive, and all she wanted to do was to have him make a commitment to her--and to be a good father to the child she was carrying. It seemed clear to me and probably many in the audience that she should just give up on this unholy relationship and put her energy into her own life, and the life of the child she carried. She hung on meekly saying, "But I love him".

The truth is she does not love herself enough to protect herself and her child from him. When I see a desperate, unholy situation like this, I know something terrible is happening. It's not about love; it's about the lack of love. This girl feels she needs this man "to feel loved". Actually, she needs his love for security, because she hasn't discovered the love within herself. This woman was clearly settling for less--a lot less than anyone deserves.

What Is A Holy Relationship?

A holy relationship is a relationship not based on differences; but a relationship based on spiritual similarities. Each partner has gone through their own personal ordeal, they have faced their own enemies, enlisted their allies and found a way to this place. They have done the inner work and found love. In looking within, each partner sees no deficiency. Within their soul, they are complete. This sense of completeness, which comes from knowing they are children of God, changes their perspective toward life and love.

By accepting this completeness of Self, each lover extends their wholeness to the other, equally as whole. They see no differences between their spiritual selves, for differences are only of the body. Therefore, they look on nothing they would take from the other. Holy partners do not come together to rob each other. They come together to let the Holy Spirit work through them.

So, how might you recognize a holy relationship? There are six characteristics: the first is there is less insecurity. Secondly, the fear of loss is lessened; third, competition is lessened; and fourth, the relational tension is lessened. Then, a new perspective emerges, and finally, God is invited to share in the relating.

Benefits of Spiritual Relating

CHARACTERISTIC #1. COMPLETENESS MEANS LESS INSECURITIES

A spiritual relationship is different from all other relationships because the spiritual completeness of each partner enables the relationship to operate with fewer insecurities. Rarely is anyone one hundred percent physically perfect, or socially adept, or intellectually and emotionally perfect. We all have flaws, of the body and of the mind. In a holy relationship, physical or intellectual imperfections do not matter because we are all spiritually perfect children of God.

Loving someone for their body is like loving a Christmas package for its wrapping. If you never have to unwrap it, you can enjoy it. If the wrapping never becomes worn or soiled, you can enjoy it. But until you unwrap it, you can never tell what is inside the pretty package. If you unwrap it, you will lose the pretty packaging--but that is the only way to get to the real thing. Loving a body is superficial--there is no "knowing"! Eventually, when the packaging is gone, you may not like the present you find inside.

We cannot be perfect in our physical beauty because it's transitory fading with age, or sickness. We can't always be perfect socially with just the right job, the right car, the right amount of money. We can't always be perfect intellectually because there is always someone who knows more than we do. Trying to be perfect causes insecurity--simply because we can't win.

But in a spiritual sense, there is one area where you are completely beautiful--within your soul. It would be difficult to imagine that anyone who is "born of God" is incomplete. Perfection comes to us only in the spiritual sense and only when we have been through some spiritual awakening and come to know and understand the value of spirit. Only when we have touched our own soul, and found the divine within can we become something new. We give up our search for human perfection, only to find perfection in our spiritual Self.

It is this sense of spiritual completeness that makes the difference in a holy relationship. Relationship now is a place where the spirit can grow, rather than a place where insecurities abound. Both partners are armed with the surety of their spiritual completeness, their spiritual invulnerability, their own one hundred percent spiritual excellence.

So, if someone we love loses their physical beauty, or their social status, or their ability to think clearly, they are still complete within their soul. A truly spiritual person never loses their belief that they are loved by God, and that they are enough. A spiritual person not only shines from within, but takes all the light that falls on them, changing it to a white radiance shot with glints of the rainbow, and spreads that light out to the world. When two spiritually mature people come together, there is more beauty and less fear of loss, less competition and less tension.

CHARACTERISTIC #2 THE FEAR OF LOSS IS LESSENED

In a spiritual relationship, you are rewarded by a relationship which is not thwarted by fears. In some relationships, the fear of abandonment can be so great that it can cause a partner to truly believe that they will die if they are not loved by their partner. There is no logic in this but it seems true to the person who fears the loss of love.

I understand this kind of reasoning because in my second marriage I gave myself away in a relationship, and felt that without that person there was nothing left. It was years before I could enter a loving relationship again. But when I did I was armed with the knowledge that I did not need anyone's love to complete myself. All I needed was the love of God within me.

That knowledge was the reward of having survived my personal ordeal, of having come to find the Love of God within me. Now, there is no competition, no tension, no inner and outer struggle in my marriage. It's just "a holy place to be!"

CHARACTERISTIC # 3 COMPETITION IS LESS

In a spiritual relationship competition is lessened. When you feel complete within, you can extend yourself to another person in a more generous way. It's not a matter of who is best because "both are best". In a spiritual sense, which is the most important consideration of all, there are no differences. In the spirit, there's perfect equality. It's not equality determined by the world with its measures and standards but an equality freely given by God. When you are born in God, who is Love, you are born into complete perfectness; therefore, there is no need to compete with anyone. Obviously I did not discover the differences between an " unholy" relationship and a "holy one" without living it.

My Relationship Story

As the second oldest of eight children, I was brought up in a typical Irish Catholic home. Both of my parents emigrated from Ireland, were very religious, and were "dry" alcoholics.

Spirituality: A Life Force

I remember them as good, loving parents who sacrificed for their children.

However, when I was fourteen years old, my father died of cancer leaving my mother with eight children from two to fifteen years old. My parents believed the church's ruling about birth control and believed that it would be sinful not to have a large family.

Even though there was a great deal of religion in my background, my idea of God was punitive and frightening. Perhaps I felt that we must have done something wrong to have inherited so much hardship. My parents carried to us the harsh superstitious beliefs and myths of Gaelic Catholicism. I even went on to graduate from a Catholic college with four years study of theology. This religion that stressed sin and repentance was all I knew.

Some of the beliefs that I brought to my adult relationships were typical of someone dealing with a spiritual void. No amount of religion seemed to help. Because I had been brought up poor and Catholic in a rich and Protestant Yankee town, I believed that I wasn't a worthwhile person.

Secondly, because my mother was a codependent caretaker, I believed that if I was to be loved that I would have to pay for it by caretaking. Third, because my father died and left my mother with eight kids, I realized my needs would not be met if I depended on someone else; and, finally, because I lost my father at age 14, I believed eventually I would be abandoned. I brought all these faulty beliefs to the relationships I entered. What I didn't know was that this lack of love on the inside was affecting my relationships.

My First Marriage

While in college, I met my first husband and married one year after graduation. We had a bright future with both of us well educated, healthy and in love. What could have been a life-long union began to deteriorate through alcoholism.

All of our drinking was camouflaged by the acceptance at the country club and an active social life, but it was the beginning of addiction for both of us. We had three healthy children and by the time they were in their early teens, I knew I couldn't stay in the marriage and stay sober, so I left! This marriage ended in divorce. My recovery from addiction began at this point in my life, but my recovery from relational problems took much longer.

My Second Marriage

After four years of recovery from alcoholism, I met a man who was also in recovery. Still I had the spiritual void within me; still I was searching for some answers to relational problems. In my former marriage, addiction had been the dominant force and it had cheated my husband and me of any relational or spiritual growth. This time I was dealing with a partner who was also in early recovery and a member of the clergy.

Because he was a senior pastor in a large parish, it seemed to me that now I had a chance for spiritual growth. We were both sober and working on ourselves spiritually or at least that is what I wanted to believe.

Spirituality: A Life Force

But what I didn't know was that my husband was "dually addicted". Having no knowledge of sexual addiction, I thought my husband's dealings with the women of the parish were a normal part of his job as pastor. He was well liked, rather charismatic, and sought after by everyone. Why shouldn't the women seek out his help. At first, I was blind sighted by the deception inherent in his using his spiritual position as a vehicle to carry out his sexual addiction.

After two years of marriage, a continuing affair with a woman from a previous church was validated. He admitted that, in truth, he did have a serious problem. After a feeble attempt to get counseling, it became clear that he suffered from a compulsion to obsessively seek out sexual encounters with women. Many on-going affairs came to light!

I saved myself and my sobriety by leaving what I perceived to be a hopeless situation; and, ultimately divorced him. Ten days after the divorce, he remarried his former wife, but continued an on-going affair with a married woman in the church whom he was sexually active with during our marriage and during his second courtship of his ex-wife. Three weeks after his re-marriage to his ex-wife, he was sued by the irate husband of that parishioner. When his sexual addiction came out in court, his church took action against him.

A Time of Spiritual Transformation

Ironically, when I left this marriage, I hit bottom! It became clear to me that I had been reaching out to others to fill in the spiritual void within me. How could I have ever been involved in such a sick relationship? What was wrong with me? This was the turning point of my life!! I was so broken, so alone that there was no place to go but to God.

In front of the church where my former husband preached was a huge sign that said "God Is Love". I came to fully understand that sign and know that no matter what happens in the material world, I will always be sustained by God. It took this humiliating loss of a marriage in a very public setting to help me grieve all the losses of my lifetime.

Since I no longer lived in the parsonage, and was no longer a member of the church, I joined another church, attended services, retreats, and began to attend meetings of *A Course In Miracles* held on Sunday mornings, as well as Bible Study on week nights. Innately, I knew that it was the spiritual side of me that needed attention. Through opening myself up to many spiritual programs, I became open to filling that spiritual void.

As I explained earlier, through *A Course In Miracles*, Bible Study, and worship services, I came to understand that I am a child of God. Up until this point in my life, I looked for my identity outside of myself and tried to fill that spiritual void with a relationship. At this point, I knew I was whole and complete within myself not needing another person to fill me spiritually. It was as complex and as simple as that!

However, my choice of partner had to be addressed. Why had I chosen addicted partners? As usual I researched and I wrote--in 1991, **Love, Infidelity and Sexual Addiction** was published. By researching that book, I realized where I had gone wrong in my partnership choices. Addiction was all I knew!

Spirituality: A Life Force

Now I sought a healthy partner and quickly withdrew from any relationship that showed any signs of unhealthy relating. In this dating experience, it became a matter of quick response, setting boundaries, and clear decision making. Difficult? Yes, but very rewarding!

By protecting myself from unhealthy situations, I was able to live in peace and accord with myself, to continue to honor myself as a child of God, and remain open for a healthy relationship. It was OK to be alone; God was with me!

My Marriage Today

In time, I met Bob, a man who also understands the love of God and who has grown to the same peaceful space spiritually. Bob is a man who puts God first, and me second, and most importantly, he's someone who understands why I have to put God first and him second. No longer do I seek the crisis, the challenge, the unattainable. I want a whole person--and so does he. Bob and I met in 1993 and were married in 1994.

As always my writing parallels my life experience, so in 1998, I published ***Holy Relationships***, released by Morehouse Publishing, presenting the guidelines, functions, and purposes of a "holy" relationship. This scripturally based gift book stressed that spiritual maturity is essential for lovers to enter into the deepest spiritual intimacy--a holy relationship. In 2007, the second edition of ***Holy Relationships*** was published.

Much of this chapter, is an updated version of the subject of spiritual relating written after many years of living with Bob.

Today, I know that love is generated from the inside out, that we never lose by giving it away, and that there's no scarcity of love. It's everywhere. In a chance meeting, in the coincidences of life and in this lifelong relationship. "Love Is" just as "Truth Is" and "God Is".

By coming to understand that "God is the Love in which we live," Bob and I keep our relationship sacred. By reading, meditation, praying, we sustain our own spiritual growth. No longer do we need another human being to sustain us. Yet, we have never been so intrinsically connected to another human being. Bob and I are inseparable in our commitment. This commitment helps us to care for one another, to communicate enough to have built a beautiful home, to develop his practice as a family therapist, and my writing career, to travel and generally live a peaceful and productive life. If I am a child of God, then I must live in Love and conduct my life in a loving way.

Through forgiveness and acceptance, I became open to the love of my husband. He's on the same spiritual plane as me and that compatibility has made this marriage sacred--a holy relationship! We view each other as children of God; we hold each other sacred. This idea of the sacredness of relationship came from an incidental conversation that Bob and I had early in our relationship. I knew that our relationship was different so I asked him what he thought made the difference. He simply said, "We hold each other sacred". Those words never left me and have become a living part of our marriage.

For those who read this book, there's a clear message of hope. You can be happy in a relationship; you can have continued success and the peace of mind that comes from healthy, spiritual relating. It's not only possible, but it's your right. All you need do is continue to grow spiritually--to find the Love within. Then, you will attract to you; one, like you who has also found the Love within. Hold each other sacred and treasure the gifts of your loving relationship, just as God treasures you. God is Love and He sustains our human love. Today and always!!

Because the perspective of the partners is different in a holy relationship, its function is different. Our actions are always affected by our beliefs or our overall view of life. So it is in spiritual relationships.

Functioning In A Spiritual Relationship: By changing my perspective of myself, by attaining a spiritual wholeness, I improve my chances of relating in a spiritual way. I bring this spiritual self to my relationship with you; I now see you as a child of God and what's so important I treat you as a child of God. If I have a negative, jaded view of myself, I may see myself as deficient, as less than others. I may not think I'm as smart, as socially adept, or as clever as others. If I don't have the connection within myself to understand my intrinsic worth; then, I may project this low self esteem outward to others. I can only see others as I see myself. The functioning in a holy relationship becomes sacred when both partners accept their spiritual place in life. So what does that mean in a practical sense of dealing with daily problems?

Return to basics: Initially, we need to return to some of the sacred precepts we knew as children. Christ said: "Let the little children come unto me." Perhaps he meant that if we wish to be more spiritual, we need to return to the basic honesty inherent in all children. We need to give ourselves permission to "ask questions when we don't know" and we need to "trust first" and "play all the time" Those are the ways of innocence, of spirituality. Society may teach us to protect ourselves with lies, or to hesitate to ask questions, or not to trust anyone, but those are the ways of society not of spirituality.

Know how to communicate: We have to learn what to say in a holy relationship and understand that not only is it natural to feel our feelings but it's important to share those feelings. We can actually say we are angry, sad, or happy in a spiritual relationship. We can't use these feelings to abuse another person, but we have the right and obligation to own them and express them in a non-threatening way.

Spiritual energy flows from partner to partner in a joining of two spirits. There is an open channel of communication; therefore, we tell each other everything that will strengthen our relationship. Like telling each other the things you are grateful for; like complementing the good you see in your partner. Every time you see it. Obviously there are sometimes when we don't tell our exact feelings if it would damage or hurt our partner or the relationship; but, in general, we share everything. We bless each other with every positive thought of each other and praise our partner, much as we praise God. Here we are not speaking of functioning with flattery, or ego inflation to win our own way. We "speak everything good" to affirm the spirit of our lover only to find we are affirmed as well. And when we miss a moment of praise, we go back to it and recreate that moment. Time can be flexible. We use it to help our partners grow spiritually by praising their sacredness. In "speaking everything good", we use every avenue of expression possible--words, touch, letters, gifts, kindnesses. We also listen to music and make it ours. We touch. We enjoy nature together. And food, and silence. As a couple, you can communicate with God together. Formal prayer serves

Spirituality: A Life Force

this purpose when you stand together in church in faith before God; however, you can initiate times of informal prayer and enriching spiritual moments as well.

Because we're human, sometimes our relationships break down. Knowing how to communicate helps fix them. There are times when it's necessary to compromise and there are times when it's OK to just laugh and be silly bringing a little frivolity to the relationship.

When anger occurs, it can become a tool for greater self-knowledge, greater spiritual growth. If we accept our anger as our own, it can lead us to know our weak points and to discover ways to heal ourselves. Anger is a great teacher if we take its power and allow it to show us what hurt lies beneath. We cannot change a relationship with anger; however, we can change ourselves by listening to our anger.

Know how to protect the relationship: Today we see people discard their "joining together" in such a casual way. Marriages are entered into too easily and divorce is all too easy an option. By making divorce the first solution, couples devalue the actual joining; they devalue the energy that flows between the two spirits as they relate. Relationships are not to be taken lightly because they serve their purpose in our development. Our relationships need protection.

We need to respect the relationship as a viable, blessed union. Society will treat any relationship as dispensable. There's little regard for the sanctity or privacy of anyone. Just watch a week of the popular talk shows. Couples on those shows have put their relationships at the mercy of strangers.

Outside people, places, and things can erode the most "sacred joining of spirits." Not every counselor is the right one for your marriage. Not every suggestion of a family member or close friend is valid for you. Not every venture out on the internet is safe. As we might protect any sacred object, we need to stay aware within the relationship learning to place the proper value on it and protect it.

Know how to function spiritually: So, as we learn to think in more spiritual terms, we learn to function in more spiritual ways. Love is not based on conditions but is unconditional. We learn to give up control of our partner and set their spirit free, and we accept, not judge them, or their actions. Many couples join together to gain material wealth, to have children, to have social recognition. These are the world's reasons for joining, but the spiritual purpose for "holding each other sacred" is that each partner might grow spiritually. In thinking about how to grow spiritually within a relationship, I think of these principles that have guided me in my marriage to Bob.

Principle One: In a holy relationship, forgiveness is the primary function. Through forgiveness of others we come to see ourselves as forgiven, as sacred. Forgiveness is the primary function for cleansing the relationship and allowing it to return to its original state of innocence. Purging out unhealthy guilt is another cleansing function of holy relationships.

Principle Two: In a holy relationship, we are aware of the spiritual growth of our partner. If I contribute to the spiritual deterioration of the one I love then I'm not loving them, I'm using them to bring harm unto themselves. That's not a holy joining together because it's parasitic, codependent, unhealthy and unholy.

Principle Three: In a holy relationship, we set and maintain boundaries. When you "hold each other sacred", you understand the need to set and maintain boundaries. As with all that is sacred, there are limits which need to be honored. We would not defile a temple set up for worship, yet some defile the bodies of their mate. We would not yell profanities inside a church, yet we yell them at our mate. There's nothing more sacred than the soul of another human; nevertheless, we allow our souls to be defiled. When you're spiritually in tune, you understand your rights, your limits and your place in the world.

Principle Four: In a holy relationship, we embrace freedom. Freedom is the natural by-product of a spiritual relationship. There are no limits on the answers you can give to your mate. You can say "no", "yes", "maybe", or "I don't know". This flexibility exists because you and your partner recognize that "growth in spirit" is progressive. There's no way that you can expect your mate to say "yes" to all requests. Because I need this flexibility, I recognize that my partner also needs room to grow; therefore, I offer the same choices to him.

But what if you disagree? That will happen but your tools for handling conflict must change. In a spiritual joining, you do not need to fight back. You hold your own sacred strength within you. On the other hand, you don't need to give in all the time either. There's no place for sulking in the corner, or passive aggression, in a holy relationship; but there's a place for negotiating, and a need for fairness. If you lose your sense of spirituality in order to be right, you are trying to fill in the blank spaces of your very being with ego and control. If you allow another to have and to express their difference of opinion, you will come to a place of negotiated agreement.

Principle Five: In a holy relationship, we celebrate the relationship with sacred rituals. Like all sacred ventures, we need ceremony, music, and symbolic gestures and objects to mark the milestones in our relationships. For a deeper kind of relating, it's necessary to pay attention to the habits of ritual in everyday living.

For example, it would be difficult to imagine the work of Gurumayi Chidvilasananda at the Siddha Yoga Meditation Ashram without the ritualistic chants which inspire feelings of devotion and longing for God. Yet, ancient rituals are not confined to the Indian Tradition, they're there for us in simpler forms in everyday relationships.

It's wise to consider how you might celebrate the spirituality of your relationship--some choose to go to church, bible study, prayer meetings, or trips to the ocean where they walk in silence. Some simply sit together watching a movie. Finding a place of peace is important. It can be a quiet stream, perhaps, the mountains. Wherever your place may be, it should be visited frequently as you progress in your spiritual relationship. Loving rituals confirm your sacredness and strengthen your intimate relationship.

Principle Six: In a holy relationship, we ask for help. All of these principles of spiritual relating seem so complex. Are they? Yes! But do they work? Yes! A holy relationship is a viable living union where positive energy is exchanged. It takes a strong commitment to maintain such a relationship and we need to ask for help.

Spirituality: A Life Force

Since you can't do everything yourself, it's necessary, to ask for help--from your partner and from God. With the Holy Spirit guiding your relationship, it will be easier to endure life's difficulties. There's more power to share when you both draw on God's power-sharing and exchanging the energy. When your relationship seems to be stalemated and in trouble, you bring God into each situation by asking for help. Say, "Dear God, heal this relationship with your love. Please help me to do my part." Then, do all that you can to heal the situation and wait and see what happens.

Chapter 6

Spiritual Purposes

When you see yourself, and your partner, as a child of God you use spiritual principles to direct the functioning of your relationship, and your relationship belongs to God. With this perspective, you can dedicate the operation of your relationship to a higher purpose. All interactions within that relationship have a new spiritual purpose, function and value. No longer do you need to think of it in an ordinary way. In a spiritual relationship, you invite God to mentor your relationship. You make contact with Him through prayer, reflection, and meditation. You rely on Him, not on yourself. A relationship progresses in a different way because God is in everything you see; God goes everywhere you go. There is nothing to fear when God is the strength in which you trust.

Under these conditions, your relationship is sustained by the love of God. There's a new freedom as you turn your relationship over to God. The demons of fear, quilt, judgment, and anger are thwarted by real love. There's no grasping, trying to fill in the soul with love, because it's already full. Love is unconditional because there are no expectations of perfection. Both people are already perfect as children of God.

With a new God-centered perspective, relationships are enriched. No longer is it acceptable to be together **just** to have children, to buy property, or to have a satisfactory sex life. These things are still within a relationship but not the primary purposes of relationship.

PURPOSE # ONE-- TO REMOVE ALL THE BARRIERS TO LOVE

All barriers to love are based in fear. So the sacred commission in a holy relationship is to seek out any and all barriers that hide beneath the surface--all the barriers within us. There may be the fear of not getting enough love, or fear of a complete loss of love, or fear of failing at love. All are rooted in childhood experience. Find the fears and remove them and you will be capable of returning the love that's inside you to another.

The fear of not getting enough love: The first fear deals with "not getting enough love." Usually, the person dealing with this fear is very needy. They may be coupled with a partner who likes to give and seems content; consequently, their neediness is not terribly apparent. However, the relating is not healthy spiritually if one person operates out of the fear of "not getting enough love" while the other has a tendency to only feel complete when they are caring for another. Spiritual growth is stagnated in this arrangement. Usually, this fear of not getting enough love comes from a childhood circumstance of "love deficiency."

Deepak Chopra said in ***A Path To Love*** "all fear is a projection from the past. You generate fearful situations to accommodate that fear. Everything you fear must have already happened or you wouldn't fear it. Spiritually, the answer to fear is that we're already safe. Safe in God's love and care."

The fear of loss of love: A fear of loss of love might result from an early death of a parent, or from absentee parenting behaviors. As a child, it's really difficult to believe that love doesn't keep disappearing when it actually does. When a parent is gone or doesn't return love to a child, the child is apt to feel unlovable. Since it's hard to erase childhood convictions, this training can be the ticket to disastrous relationships in the future.

Believing that your relationship will end any moment is not particularly conducive to establishing and maintaining a peaceful, productive long term relationship. You may see every normal disagreement as the beginning of the divorce proceeding. You may trigger discontent by distrusting the permanence of the relationship. This kind of fear can set up inordinately excessive demands for reassurance.

The fear of failing at love: A fear of failing at love sets up a tentative "joining together". Whenever you are beset by fears of not being able to succeed in relationships, you tread lightly. There is a tendency to be less than honest so as not to offend, to be negligent in establishing your priorities, to deny yourself your rights within the relationship--even to the point of "people-pleasing" all the time.

A tentative, unsure position is never a good position to have in the joining of two people. The one who fears failure is bound to give in too much, to sabotage their own needs and possibly feel cheated and even exploited. The one who lives with this partner gets into a pattern of expectations and entitlement. Then a sense of guilt of guilt when they realize there is inequity.

Love produces a bold, active energy! A holy relationship demands equal energy from equal partners who are sure of their identity as God's children, complete within themselves.

PURPOSE # TWO -- TO TEACH LOVE

God is Love! You are His child.! You are from Love, itself; therefore, your purpose is to teach what you are. How do you do that? Just ask, "Is This The Loving Thing To Do? Sometimes the most loving thing to do is the most difficult. To honestly approach a delicate issue with another person, even when you're afraid, is a loving thing to do.

For example, your lover has made a remark about another person and you wonder if you are being compared in an unfair way. You hurt inside. What do you do? Forget it? Let it simmer? Try to talk yourself out of the hurt? The loving thing to do is to gently tell the truth, "When you said that I felt hurt." Gently ask them to clarify what they meant by saying what they said. "Did you mean by that remark to suggest that your sister is more considerate to you than I am?' "Are you saying I need to work on being more considerate?" Ask for clarification and expect to get answers.

If your partner sees you in a spiritual way, they'll be able to see the hurt and wish to clarify the issue. If they're defensive, they are seeing only their own situation and perhaps feel criticized. Be prepared to ask gently and to accept whatever they say. You may hear that one of the best qualities of this sister is a considerate nature. Accept this. But if your lover has any complaints about your consideration, they need to speak up at this time. This is the loving way to approach things. Compromising, apologizing or admitting wrong can maintain mutual spiritual health.

Immediacy and firmness are important in confronting delicate issues. Stand firm whenever your spiritual growth is being hampered by the circumstances. But be willing to see where you might have gone wrong too. To compromise, to apologize and say "I was wrong" are loving things to do.

The final question is always a spiritual one. Does this act help me or harm me spiritually? Does this act help or harm my partner's spirituality? Maintaining your mutual spiritual health is "the loving thing to do".

PURPOSE # THREE -- TO COMMUNICATE WITH GOD

The third purpose of a holy relationship is to communicate with God on a regular basis. Communicate means direct contact through prayer. Does that mean that you need to be on your knees praying for a good part of the day. No, not at all. But it does mean that your mind remembers God as you function throughout the day. If you are living a spiritual life most of your day will be prayerful in and of itself.

Prayer can be formal or informal. Formal prayers are important because the ritual of the religious service can publicly make a statement to the world about your intentions to live a holy life, and witness your dedication to God. However, most prayer is informal. Informal prayer is every thought we have, and every word we say. It shows through in the grateful caring attitude we carry with us each day.

For example, you pray when you let your mind reach out to God as you drive to work, or just before you sleep. "Mind-references" to God are prayers. You pray when you tone down an angry impulse--perhaps when a car cuts in front of you. You can mentally pray for the driver as they speed off saying, "God be with them." Turn them and their behavior over to God and go on in peace.

Informally praying together as a couple can be a powerful tool for a holy relationship. It rededicates both of you to God and reminds each partner of the higher purposes of the relationship. It can be as simple as listing in prayer all the things you are grateful for, or all your concerns, or all the people you wish to lift up to God.

Many opportunities to bond together in prayer are missed simply because we don't make it a habit to pray informally together. We simply forget. I suspect if more people knew the power of such experiences, they would cultivate "relationship prayer."

PURPOSE # FOUR--TO PRACTICE FAITH

Faith is evidenced when we turn our life and will over to the care of God. We do this when we dedicate all the actions of our life and our relationships to God. Where do we start? First, we come to believe in God as a loving God not a punishing one. This conviction is essential. Many people were brought up in religions which teach that if you sin "God will get you." In that environment, it's easy to forget the primary quality of God is love.

Spirituality: A Life Force

So, if you have a negative vision of God, you'll need to change that perspective believing that God is on your side. You can't have faith in a God that is punitive and remain comfortable. Belief in a benevolent God that wants the best for you is the core of all faith. Once you understand a loving God, you're willing to let God into your heart and your holy relationship.

Practicing faith simply means turning over your will to God. Trusting in the goodness of the universe, having hope in all things. When we are met with some disappointment or sorrow, God asks only one thing--**acceptance**. We don't have to understand the situation, or like it. In the case of some seemingly unnecessary tragedy, we may even work hard to see that it never happens again. However, to rail against God, or to blame God is not the position of a person of faith. We must accept life as it is.

A person of faith is willing to depend on God in times of trouble; to wait and see what good might come from the misfortune; to trust that there will be some good. Basically, to be willingly open--minded and humble enough to believe that not all answers are on the surface of the event. In our humanness we can't possibly see the whole picture. But God can and will guide us, bringing the good out in our lives. In Proverbs (3:5,6) it says "Trust in the Lord with all your heart, and lean not on your own understanding: in all ways acknowledge Him, and He shall direct your path." These words spring to life for those who have come to know the Love of God.

There are many times when a blind trust in God is necessary to function in life and in your relationships. If you were to try to understand all that you see in the world, that is, the senseless tragedy, and general pain of life, you might come to believe that God has made a meaningless world. But God could not make a meaningless world. Just because we do not have the ability to understand the vagaries of life does not mean that there's no greater meaning.

If we make God our primary source of power and love, we will be able to let go of some of the questions we have of the world. Especially when we don't understand. Christ said, "I am the vine, you are the branches. He who abides in Me, and I in Him, bears much fruit; for without Me you can do nothing". (John 15:5 NKJV) With this new perspective of hope and bounty, our relationships become holy and flourish.

We can't possibly trust our humanness for carrying out our sacred calling in spiritual relationships. This work is greater than human forces. We need to look to a higher power. If we believe in the power of God, we can come to believe in the power of ourselves, through God, and in the power of others, through God, and in the power of our relating.

Once you have adopted a position of faith in God within you, you can extend this faith to yourself and another. ***If you're in a spiritual relationship, the best way to keep your love alive and growing ever deeper is to give God your relationship as a gift.*** Ask God to protect your relationship from all that would separate you from your ultimate good.

Whenever a problem arises in the relationship, give it to God and you will find solutions that are more perfect and complete. Faith in your relationship means that you are willing to surrender to God, to be shown a better way. The best way is always the perfect answer--where both partners are respected as children of God. Ask for help to find these solutions.

Spirituality: A Life Force

As Joan Gattuso said in ***A Course In Love*** "meeting your soulmate may be one of the first steps to living in a holy relationship blessed every instant by love, but it isn't the last step. Now the two of you can walk together hand-in-hand to God."

There are times when a blind trust is necessary in relationship. In a time of crisis it's very easy to revert to old fears that might cause reactive behaviors. You might begin to fear that things won't work out for you, or that some incident could destroy your loving relationship. When there is a death in the family, when someone loses their job, when someone is sick: these are particularly difficult times. Sometimes a complete trust in the relationship is needed to help us understand that the relationship will not fail just because life produces critical changes.

PURPOSE # FIVE--TO OFFER FORGIVENESS

Forgiveness may not be easy--especially when you feel betrayed. But it's essential because it cleanses you not the other person. Our primary function in life is to forgive others so that we might live in peace ourselves. At one time in my life, if I had I not internalized the idea that "forgiveness is a gift to me," I might never have loved again. For some reason we think of forgiveness as a kind of prize that we may or may not give whenever we choose. Not extending forgiveness fosters resentment within us. It's not conducive to our spiritual health.

If you don't forgive, conflict will dominate your relationships. Your ultimate goal is always peace of mind through forgiveness. By adding the element of forgiveness to any relationship you leave your partner's soul intact. You were never meant to condemn or judge--just forgive. Sometimes partners feel like if they forgive they will have to submit to further wrongs. That's not true. You can forgive without condoning the wrong doing. After having confronted the issue, a new solution needs to be found. New boundaries are set, but first there must be forgiveness.

Forgiveness is a part of "I love you". It's not a positioning that allows one person to feel better than another. It's the primary function of all relationships; it's the decision to enter a process of healing and to go on with loving. Forgiveness is the key to a happy ending in any confrontation because it opens up a new chapter in the relationship. We all know that when we forgive ourselves, we can start over again. When we forgive our partner, we open the relationship to love again. We offer this new beginning to our lover--just as we take it for ourselves in self-forgiveness.

Forgiveness is our primary function and the means whereby we find our way to peace of mind. Why hold back? Some people believe forgiveness is a gift to those who seemed to have harmed us. It isn't! Forgiveness is always a gift to self. Holding back forgiveness simply means we are stuck in the "blaming stages" of forgiveness. Release of another person through forgiveness is release of self!

There are many holy instances in our lives! Moments that are somehow touched by the holy spirit-moments of intense healing. We can appreciate those moments as we forgive, as we search for healing. No one can ever know when they will experience such a powerful spiritual realization. Sometimes it happens in an instant.

It happened to me when I heard a sermon one Sunday morning. In speaking of forgiveness, the minister said, "**the forgiveness you are seeking to give has already happened in the mind and heart of God. It is up to you whether you want to acknowledge it here in this life or in the next."**

I was greatly affected by that statement and decided to forgive my second husband of his many infidelities fueled by sexual addiction. I asked to meet him. In the following fictionalized narrative, I describe that meeting:

She crossed the Piccard Bridge as the onslaught of four o'clock traffic broke loose. It was hot and her silk dress clung to her back. Her temples were wet--a single rivulet of water made its way down her neck.

Perhaps I should have said six o'clock she thought. Then we could have avoided the traffic. Screeching brakes stunned Jenny as she closed in on the car in front of her. "Never mind I know this is right", she said aloud. "This is what I have to do!"

Over the Piccard Bridge jersey barriers, through the construction for a mile, and; finally the traffic broke out of its cadence like a child anxious to be free.

She was nervous! She admitted it, it was true! It had been two months since she had seen him and she heard he would remarry his first wife next month. Bitter thoughts of betrayal and hurt crowded in as an angry motorist beeped at Jenny. To move on! Yes, to move on she thought. He didn't give me much leeway she thought. They will be remarried ten days after our divorce. Again, anger and resentment welled up in her.

"It's not for me to judge, I'm accountable for my thoughts and actions", she said. Somehow her inner reassurances helped her to go on. Yesterday, when Jenny called Paul's office to ask for this meeting there was hostility in his voice but he agreed to meet at the restaurant. Now, Jenny wondered if he would break into anger here. Or, would she become silent and unable to speak? As she neared the restaurant, she wondered if she could sit down with a man who had been her husband, betrayed her, and would soon remarry his first wife.

"I'm not sure of what I am doing", she muttered as she turned into the parking lot. She saw his car. With a deep breath she straightened her jacket, another deep breath and she entered the restaurant.

Her last thought was a prayer that she could do what she had come to do. Smiling, she walked to the back of the restaurant where Paul was waiting. For a few minutes she said nothing! Neither did he! She continued to smile! Suddenly, there was a calm within her. No hurry--just peace.

"I am happy to be sharing the same space with you".

"What?" he questioned taken back by her calm. Her loving comment caught him off guard and he looked like he might cry. There was an awkward moment.

"I am happy to be here with you," she repeated, still smiling. "I just mean that it feels good to be sharing the same space with you." More silence!

Finally, he agreed, adding, "You look good!"

"I am good", she said. No response. A waitress asked if she wanted coffee. Jenny nodded affirmatively while the woman placed the cup on the table and filled it.

Spirituality: A Life Force

Motioning toward Paul's cup the waitress said, "More coffee?" Paul nodded and smiled saying, "It's always over coffee, isn't it? Some things never change." They both laughed.

Over coffee, Jenny began to address the issue at hand. She spoke of her part in their marriage reiterating where she felt she had gone wrong. Not once did she refer to what he had done.

Defensive tears came to him because he had not expected this. The power of her defenselessness was overpowering!! Soon, he began a burst of amends.

"But I was wrong. I am the one to ask for forgiveness," he interjected almost in frenzy. "I need to ask you to forgive me!"

"No you don't! It is already done! The reconciliation between you and me has already taken place in the mind and heart of God. All we need to do catch up, to recognize what already is", she said.

After a long silence he nodded his understanding and smiled again. She returned the smile and repeated, "I am happy to be able to share this space with you today!"

Yes! I am too." he answered.

The space of forgiveness shared that day was special, even sacred! The booth with its leather seats, the floor with its grease stains, and the diligent waitress are probably still there; but, somehow that space will never be the same. It's like that with forgiveness. There's power in defenselessness--it's louder than silence, it leaves an everlasting mark. It's our primary function in all our human relationships!

There's a great deal of room in our thought system for condemnation of certain behaviors while preserving the sanctity of the individual. We're not ever saying that we agree with the behavior. But it's not our job to absolve anyone of the harm they inflicted on us, or those we love. Absolving is a judgment act and a positioning of the ego. Absolving says "I am better, you are less." We don't absolve; we simply recognize the underlying sanctity of another child of God.

When forgiveness becomes our primary function, we accept the challenges of life in a loving way. In this stance, there's no spiritual separation. If I am a child of God, forgiven of all past errors; then, so are you. Love holds no grievances, so neither can I.

By choosing to hang onto old hurts, we can remain victims. People may feel sorry for us and we might not have to be as responsible as we could be. After all, we have undergone "great trauma." Why shouldn't we be given a little leeway? There's an illusion of being the "good guy" when you're the victim. God loves us all. There are no "good guys" or "bad guys" just forgiven children of God. This is the time to actively drop the victim role and embrace healing–it's a time to forgive.

By staying in my ego, I can remain "right" in all situations of my life. Life becomes a battle to prove I'm better than you--more right! You are 100% wrong in a given situation and I will prove it! That kind of thinking keeps all hurts alive. It's useless to reenact the creation of the wound. We all suffer injury in life and healing those wounds is more important than rehashing the circumstances of the hurt. If I could live my life without hurting others, I would be "superhuman." There's much harm that's done inadvertently by all of us.

Spirituality: A Life Force

By looking at forgiveness as a weakness rather than strength, we can adapt a false position of strength and "never give in." We think we're showing that other person that they can't get away with hurting us. In reality, we are keeping the wound open and unhealed. An open, unhealed wound continues to poison us. Life is not a matter of personal power over others. It's more a matter of connecting with the power within us.

PURPOSE # SIX -- TO HEAL AND BE HEALED

In **The Marriage Spirit: Finding The Passion And Joy Of Soul-Centered Love,** Drs. Evelyn and Paul Moschetta explain that any unresolved bit of unfinished business within your relationship that needs healing will take away from your love. They claim you can consciously seek out those bits of unresolved anger and resentment and clear them up with this exercise:

A Healing Dialogue: *Set aside at least an hour. Sit comfortably together and hold hands. Holding hands reminds you of what you are doing-- coming together. Speak to each other as if you will never get this chance again. This is the only time. Now.*

Follow these instructions: 1. Each of you is to go within and recall an anger which you feel is still unfinished. It can be the same issue or a different one. What matters is that healing occurs today. 2. Take turns listening to the other's story. 3. Talk about the incident. Talk about the hurt you felt then and perhaps still feel today. Talk about yourself, your thoughts and feelings. Do not get into the motives or behavior of your partner. Stay with "I statements". Don't attach blame. 4. When it is your turn to listen. Listen. Don't interrupt. Try to hear the feelings beneath the facts. 5. Don't let your mind wander. Bring it back to the issue. 6. When your partner finishes say, "Let me tell you what I heard you say." Give your full understanding of what was said. Then ask, "Have I understood you?" Listen to any clarification made. 7. Verify if your partner feels that you truly understand. Then apologize. Apologize for the pain your words or actions caused. No excuse just an apology! 8. After each has told his or her story, give the gift of forgiveness. Tell the other that you will not hold onto the hurt. Let it go. 9. End each healing session by saying how happy you are to have each other in your lives.

The healing of mind, body, and spirit is a natural result of spiritual relating. However, as was demonstrated with this exercise, there are some actions that have to be taken to enable healing to take place. Both people must exercise a spiritual intention as they come together to heal.

By seeing God in another person you allow God, or love, to touch them. Love heals! That is what soul touching is all about. Your spiritual intention is to see God in your lover, and consequently in everyone you meet. Earlier in this book, I mentioned Ashley Smith and the remarkable incident where she was able to love Brian Nichols--a killer, who was touched by her love and surrendered to the authorities peacefully.

Thomas Moore In **Soulmates** suggests "the courage required to open one's soul to express itself or to receive another is infinitely more demanding than the effort we put into avoidance of intimacy." It seems easier to avoid situations like the healing exercise just described. It is. Rilke wrote, "For one human being to love another human being: that is perhaps the most difficult task that has been entrusted to us, the ultimate task, the final test and proof, the work for which all other work is mere preparation." Yes, healing is work.

Seeing your partner as a child of God affirms the love within them. Anger brings, anger. Resentment brings resentment. Bitterness brings bitterness. Love generates love and love heals.

Healing can be of the body too. There is much research today that supports the truth that love can speed recovery from illness. Doctors who have usually taken a scientific approach are now becoming more open to spiritual healing.

A book called ***Anatomy Of the Spirit: The Seven Stages Of Power and Healing*** actually combines scientific medical research with the spiritual to show the correlation. It speaks of spiritual causes of disease and makes a case for holistic healing. Books like these only reaffirm what spiritual leaders have known all along. Love does heal.

In ***The Beloved: Relationship As A Path To Awakening Embracing***, Stephen and Ondea Levine speak from personal experience of the healing exercises they have brought into their marriage. In battling with cancer, and other sickness, they worked together praying as a couple that they might "send forgiveness instead of fear into the pain." They learned to respond to bodily hurt with compassion instead of anger. And it has worked for them.

Couples can come to understand that two hearts can be blended into one healing force. There can be collaboration in healing. No longer is it isolated, individual, but focused on a shared body, and a shared heart. Learning to heal together is one of the divine purposes of a holy relationship.

PURPOSE # SEVEN--TO KNOW PEACE

The most precious gift you can bring to a relationship is your own sense of peace. Once you have experienced a new spirituality, you are capable of experiencing "true ecstasy". As Deepak Chopra states in **The Path To Love,** "spiritual ecstasy is not a feeling or an idea but a shift in perception in which direct contact with the spirit is made".

Being in ecstasy doesn't have to express itself through intensity of any kind. Chopra continues to say, "To promote stillness is to promote ecstasy." He explains that the inner being doesn't have to be tricked or manipulated to achieve stillness. Our minds are like runners that only have to slow down in order to walk; then slow down from the walk to standing still. This process of "shifting down" happens during meditation because it takes the mind from its superficial, restless state to its deeper nature--peace.

Your transformation to a more peaceful state is a gift to you and to those around you. As Joseph Campbell explained in **The Power of Myth,** "the aim of the quest must be neither release nor knowing ecstasy for oneself, but the wisdom and power to serve others. Knowing God, knowing self, knowing others,-- knowing ecstasy. When your own spiritual self-realization dawns there's no longer a question of struggle, effort, conflict. "When you have found peace within, peace becomes the very foundation

Spirituality: A Life Force

of your life. And all things are eventually realized in relationship--in our families and society itself.

Peace is your primary purpose as you function each day. Look at the fabric of your relationship. Do you seem to be fighting for the sake of fighting? Has it become a sport? Something that you do when things get a little boring? Unnecessary conflict erodes the sacredness of your relationship making it difficult for the settlement of real issues. It's hard to distinguish what is meaningful when there is conflict over everything.

From birth, our culture starts to work on us. As long as we live by the pull of the world, we will never feel peace. Jon Mundy in **Listening To Your Inner Guide**, states that "We want to be at peace, and we know there must be something more. An inner voice reminds us to wake up and remember Self, and come home again." The child in us reaches for God. We are all eternally innocent--children of God. The memory of this eternal innocence is always within us, still affecting us, calling us to peace. We can remember who we are at any moment. We need do nothing. Just be still an instant and let the world recede from us, let valueless ideas cease to have value in our restless minds, and hear the voice of God and know peace.

Just try this practice. When you feel agitated just stop for an instant--just be still an instant. Try this at any moment during the day. In the stillness of that instant you will be enfolded in perfect gentleness. That is peace.

So it is the purpose of a holy relationship to know peace and by knowing peace to give it to your lover. Christ said, "Peace I leave you: my peace I give you. I do not give as the world gives. Do not let your heart be troubled and do not be afraid." (John

14:27 NIV) We realize that promise when we pay close attention to our inner voice, when we're still for an instant and listen to our spirit. Again, we need to do nothing but accept who we truly are, God's children, and accept life as it is.

PURPOSE # EIGHT TO EXPERIENCE JOY

Most couples do not "expect" joy to inherently be a part of their relationship. They might look for moments of joy but don't understand that God's will for them is joy. It would be difficult to see a loving God as having any other purpose for us. They might ask, "Why do bad things happen? Why did our child die? Or a child was never born? Or born deformed? We don't know the answer to these questions. Except that life is full of vagaries, inconsistencies, and mysteries. We can never know "why". All we can do is to accept life as it is. "And we know that all things work together for good to them that love God, to them who are called according to his purpose." (Romans 8:28)

Always ask, "What is the joy of the moment?" Perhaps it is what we learn from the tragedy. Perhaps it is the appreciation we develop for all children when we have none of our own. Perhaps it is the process of grief and the courage to go on that gives us strength at a later time. Our struggle may become an example to others. How can good come from a bad thing? We don't know but it always does. Having faith to find and accept that goodness returns us to a place of joy. Does it make the loss any easier? No. But it defines life in a different way -- a way that gives meaning to things we cannot understand.

Spirituality: A Life Force

Acceptance of life and promotion of your own joy is crucial to developing, and maintaining, a holy relationship. ***Finding your own joy is your own task because it is never the job of your lover to make you happy.*** They may make you very happy but it is not their job. Do the inner work necessary for you to maintain happiness. Nurture your soul. Pray. Meditate. When you're not happy in your relationship, you're to blame.

When you find your own joy, you give it to others. There's nothing like living with a spiritually connected person who is joyful unto themselves. You are relieved of the responsibility of "making them happy". Happiness is a natural component in a holy relationship. All the time? Why not? As long as you can accept life as it is, remembering not to blame, or judge, you can be joyful. No one can find happiness while attempting to make their partner feel guilty, or by blaming them for their misery.

But what if you are grieving some loss and feel sad? There is joy in grief. A sense of completion, a celebration of an ending. There is joy in knowing you are free enough in spirit to grieve.

Earlier in my present marriage, Bob was laid off from his job, after thirty years with the company. Sometimes he went to the park during lunch and cried. At noon each day, when I thought of him crying in the park, I was filled with compassion and wanted to do something to take his grief away. I thought I'd write him a loving note, or buy him a gift. Then, I realized what I was doing. I was trying to remove from him the natural process of grief--trying to make it better. So, I did nothing.

Later when we talked about it, he said he was so glad that I did not react. First, it would have intimated that he was incapable of handling his grief, and perhaps that his emotions were somehow "wrong"; and it would not have allowed him the comfort of his feelings. Later, when it got close to the last day of work for him, I stepped out of the way and let him have space to grieve.

This incident taught me a great lesson in appreciation. First, that my husband is so healthy that he can share a portion of his sadness with me without fearing my interference; and, secondly, that he's a man who can accept a serious loss in a healthy way, and grieve it appropriately. We have a bond, a pact that allows us to give enough space to feel our feelings--and we don't need to feel responsible for making someone else happy all the time. God's will for me is joy; that is,--if I can accept the losses along the way--grieve and move on. It's the same for my husband. Why should I deny him his spiritual progress?

When I retired from teaching to write full time, I went through a similar process. There were sad moments when I thought of losing a connection with my students. I accepted this loss because my students had taught me love for many years. But I also knew that love does not end in them. The loss was there but I was still joyful, because I knew that God wants me to be happy. I knew there would be a new calling, new joys.

My husband has always been there to support me, and I have supported him, to share in the grieving process. Not to compensate in any way for the loss, or to assuage each other, but to simply understand. Through honest communication, that's how a holy and happy relationship functions through difficult, sad times.

Chapter 7

Spiritual Healing

As I stated in Chapter three, understanding my true nature as a child of God was essential in making the choice to live a more spiritual life. Then, it was up to me to change old behaviors and adopt new rules for living. Seeing myself as a child of God, I no longer accepted being treated in a disrespectful way, or allowed myself to engage in self-abuse. Finally, I spoke to myself with positive affirmations--making discipline my commanding force of love and making contact with God through prayer and meditation. My spiritual Self began to be more evident to me. By seeking to complete myself in some other person or thing, I had lost my True self. I came to understand that Ego is always identified with some material form. What remained when the Ego was stripped away was the deeper true "I"-- my spiritual self.

Essentially, I began to experience a new dimension of consciousness as a result of loss--of a marriage, a spouse, social position, and reputation. When it was all gone, the anguish and fear I initially felt gave way to a sacred sense of Presence, a deep peace and serenity with a freedom from fear. I had lost it all and was alone with God. That was my spiritual awakening!

Christine A. Adams

As Fr. Richard Rohr says in **Falling Upward: A Spirituality for the Two Halves of Life,** "most people's concerns remain those of establishing their personal (or superior) identity, and perhaps linking to what seems like significant people and projects" in the first part of their life. This is only half-of-life as Father Rohr sees it. There is a further journey--a spiritual awakening.

He continues, " I believe that God gives us a soul, our deepest identity, our true Self, our unique blueprint. We are given a span of life to discover it, to choose it, and to live our own destiny to the full. We do not create our souls; we "grow " them up. And, we grow spiritually much more by doing it wrong than by doing it right."

Michael Jones said in **The Seven Victories of the Divine Child,** "the yearning for answers is often heightened after we have experienced some painful event in our lives. One positive outcome of pain is that it appears to split us wide open in such a way that it opens the door for us to strive to gain some real deeper meaning of God and Spirit".

When a person has been awakened spiritually, seeing themselves as a child of God, they begin to put the "things" of the Ego aside. In addition, discerning God's message, they begin to share the Love of God, living a grateful, purpose-driven life. The example of Ashley Smith in her dealings with Brian Nichols used in earlier chapters clearly demonstrates this point.

The spiritually awakened person heals by giving away what God has given them. Ashley had been moved spiritually by reading Rick Warren's book, **The Purpose Driven Life**. Lovingly, she shared her words, her story of her spiritual awareness with a man who had just killed several people. He

Spirituality: A Life Force

listened! Brian Nichols did not understand his own "spiritual sickness" but he heard her story. Ashley did not directly heal his sick mind but reminded him of the remedy God had already given him. As a teacher of God, she gave away what God had given her.

Although there are many ways to heal, this chapter discusses three primary ones--healing through the power of words, the power of forgiveness, and the power of prayer.

1. Healing Through the Power of Words

Words heal! Throughout the ages, words have been written as an expression of truth. The greatest of all words are represented in the Bible, the Koran, the Talmud, IChing. For many years, Christians have relied on the scared words of the Holy Bible to heal and comfort them. Most Christian spiritual leaders quote from the Bible in services across the world. Islamic spiritualists and laymen go to the sacred Koran repeating the words of the Koran in daily prayer. The Jewish faithful read words of comfort and peace in the Talmud. Buddhists turn to I Ching and the Tao for healing.

For me, and for millions the words of the modern sacred writing, ***A Course In Miracles,*** bring solace. The words of the Course open the heart to healing and hope, to enlightenment and to love. In the words of the Course, it seems a great spiritual power embraces us and brings us home.

Marianne Williamson wrote in the forward of ***Accept This Gift*** by Frances Vaughan and Roger Walsh: "For me, and for millions of other people, *A Course In Miracles* is a miracle in itself--paragraph after paragraph of words that change our minds. Where we viewed the world through the eyes of fear, suddenly we see new hope revealed. Reading we are startled by its simplicity and awed by the scope of its promise....we are in the process, through exposure to these ideas on whatever level, of transforming our lives from fear to love."

A *Course In Miracles* is a cultural and publication phenomenon. Since its publication in 1976, millions of copies have been sold. Not through the promotion of a major publisher but the Course has found a growing audience through word of mouth. Dr Helen Schulman is said to have been the scribe for this channeled work which is comprised of a text, a workbook for students, and a Manual for teachers. The workbook includes 365 lessons, one for each day of the year.

Tara Singh whose work, *A Course In Miracles A Gift For All Mankind* sees "*A Course In Miracles* as the first scripture to offer a step by step curriculum for undoing the patterns of thought which keep us separated from God, ourselves and each other." *A Course In Miracles* challenges us to transform the way we perceive everything and everyone-- including ourselves.

Yet, *The Course* is not a program for self-improvement; rather it helps us undo everything that blinds us to our own perfection. *ACIM* is not an idea. It's not abstract. Its words are uttered from the actuality of the state of love. And the purpose of these words is to bring us to Love. Love is a state uncontaminated by words but words can direct us to it. There's great power in words!

Spirituality: A Life Force

Learning and teaching are one! I could not use my words to write this book if I had not first experienced the words of *A Course In Miracles*. The love of those words transformed my thinking so that I could become transformed spiritually. "Remember always what you believe you will teach." *ACIM* states. Then, as we teach, we strengthen our beliefs in the sharing of them.

"Everything you teach you are learning. Teach only love, and learn that love is yours and you are love." (*ACIM*) We teach only love because we believe that we are God's children, and we come from Love, Itself! So much of my experience with *ACIM* has been a synergistic consumption of words in stillness and peace with no expectation of learning; therefore it's difficult to write about it. Words are beyond the physical world, spiritual words defy analysis because they stand on their own. It's not enough to say they heal and free us because they do it by igniting our spirits to awareness--staying within us, breathing for us, touching others with our peace and gentleness, and allowing us to internalize our true identities as children of God.

Whenever I read in *ACIM*, just as when I read *The Holy Bible*, I am moved to a spiritual place. However, no one can possibly read T*he Course* like most other books. It's not a book to "get into" and read cover to cover. I experienced it over many readings, many years. Like The Bible, these three volumes are there for a lifetime of assimilation, of consumption, of translation into our everyday lives.

The Course relates to me directly addressing the yearning in me--to know God, to know truth, and to know peace and love. It deals with issues I have to face within myself, and it challenges me to undo the past. It allows me direct access to spiritual truths.

I become a light unto myself by becoming free from all the "knowing". I become wise to a God-created world. The words of the *A Course In Miracles* liberate me from a materialistic, ego-centered thought system and bring me a new consciousness.

The same consciousness Eckhart Tolle describes in *A New Earth: Awakening To your Life's Purpose* in this quote: "The change goes deeper than the content of the mind, deeper than your thoughts. In fact, at the heart of the new consciousness lies the transcendence of thought, the new found ability of rising above thoughts of realizing a dimension within yourself that is infinitely more vast than thought. You then no longer derive your identity, your sense of who you are, from the incessant stream of thinking that in the old consciousness you take to be yourself."

In other words, we are not the voice in our heads. We are the one who observes the thoughts--like awareness prior to thought, the space where the thought, emotion, sensation happens. This consciousness tells me I do not have to depend on others because my awakening begins within. I'm not dependent because I'm important in myself; I'm sustained by the love of God. Consciously, I say to myself: "God is the mind in which I think." "God is the Love in which I live."

With *A Course In Miracles*, I came to know perfection-- my own divine perfection as a child of God. I found freedom in that realization: a freedom that brought the stillness of a mind at peace. Just saying the words of ACIM won't work but bringing these words to a centered place of stillness within will solve all the problems of the material world. The spiritual always transcends the physical; and so it is with the powerful words of *A Course In Miracles*.

Spirituality: A Life Force

By bringing those powerful words of love into you and allowing them to awaken within you a new light, you can light the way for others. Love is never static. It flows from one being to another. Love energizes itself by sharing because by living-in-love we teach others about love. This movement of love is a healing force. In 1993, I published an entire book called ***Living In Love*** on this very subject.

Spiritual healing happens when teachers heal by giving away what God has given them. In researching my writing, I read the words of spiritual teachers like Wayne Dyer or Eckhart Tolle and I heard the words taught in ***A Course In Miracles*** *and* ***The Holy Bible*** Words are the spiritual tools for all teachers.

We are told in the words of ***The Course*** that all of us are messengers teaching either love or fear. We will extend out to others what we perceive within: "Everyone teaches and teaches all the time. This is the responsibility you inevitably assume the moment you accept any premise at all, and no one can organize his life without some thought system. Once you have developed a thought system of any kind, you live by it, and you teach it." (***ACIM*** Text 84)

Recognizing The Power of Our Everyday Words

A Course In Miracles made me realize the power of words not only in the spiritual sense but in the real world. Realizing how I had changed as a result of the words of ACIM, I came to understand the power of words in my everyday encounters with others. Since we can't see the physical damage done by words, we sometimes forget their force. Words can build from a positive energy, or can destroy with a negative force.

You may remember when you were seven years old and your aunt yelled at you for burning the pillowcase with the iron: you cringed in shame, never forgetting the feeling of failure. Ironing was her thing, she knew how to do it; you didn't, and you made a terrible mistake. Later that day, you ran to a secret place and cried, wishing you could die because you were so ashamed. It was such a simple thing but her words never left your mind.

How often do we remember one cutting remark? And, how often do we remember one expression of love? How often do we hear from others that they appreciated our words of encouragement or praise? Words are powerful because they can influence us. They can be instruments of spiritual growth or destruction; they can project love or fear. Some people think power is in fists, or bullets, or in bombs. I believe power is in words.

Not only can words shame a soul, pierce a mind, or uplift the heart in a few seconds, but they can stay with you a life time. We remember what others say to us. We remember! Remember the words of your mother when she said, "It's malignant. The doctor said it's malignant." Yes, you remember the words and the green corridors, the white tiled floors, the doors that swing open and the sign that said, Maine General Hospital. Somehow, at twelve years old, words like "malignant" never leave your mind. Or when, you picked up the telephone and again it was your mother's voice. She simply said, "I have bad news, Michael is dead." Or the words of your husband, sitting by your bed with his hands holding his head waiting for you to wake up so he could say, "The baby is dead." No one could have said words of more power--these words get branded into our minds forever.

Do you remember the first time a boyfriend or girlfriend said, "I love you."? Do you remember your response? Do you remember a favorite fourth grade teacher who told you that you could write very well, or that you were creative? Not only are words the creators of love and confidence; but they are the energy that allow us to continue to love, to work, and to create. We remember Words!

Listen To Your Words: In any spiritual healing there is a new awareness. First, I had to be healed by the power of the words of *The Bible*, the *IChing, A Course In Miracles* and other great readings; then, I had to apply this new awareness to my own use of words. The first step was to listen to my own words very carefully.

So I needed to look at my everyday words. I needed to respect their power and use them carefully. Verbal abuse, ridicule, derision, and sarcasm are the words of the ego. They are the words that say, "I am right and you are wrong." "I am better, you are less." "I am afraid of you so I will make you less than me." Words hurt! Negative words separate and destroy the loving spirits of others.

In loving personal relationships, I needed to check my own words. How did I sound? Loving? Or fearful? Righteous? What was my agenda? What did my words really mean? I have to remind myself to listen to what I'm saying and that will establish where I am spiritually. Sometimes I fail miserably in this endeavor and I can only hope that I remain alert remembering the power of words. Having taught high school for 32 years, I realized that I could encourage or crush a student with words. Sometimes the ability to use them effectively has been both a curse and a blessing.

Words that Teach Fear: When we use words to teach fear, we are operating from our ego--based thinking. We believe we are alone in a frightening world and that we need do everything possible to protect ourselves from harm. When someone attacks us, we retaliate with words; we strike back at the mind of the attacker with hateful, angry words. In those instances, we are teaching fear, isolation, and hatred with words. Attacking anyone, at any time with words is an ego--based position of defense which says, "You are not stronger than I am." "You cannot harm me!" Defensive words may seem appropriate and necessary at times, but, in truth, they serve no useful purpose.

When we use words to make someone less, we do not believe that we are one, all equal in God's Love. There's no need for words of ridicule, sarcasm, or derision when you teach only love. These words will not change the spiritual value of our enemy because these people are equal in God's mind. It doesn't matter whether you say these hateful words anonymously online or by confronting them in person, they are His children also. Words cannot change this truth. The ego evaluates and makes less or more, but Love makes one.

Loving words that are not always what they seem: Words that sound loving are not always based in love. Since words are so powerful, people can use them to project love when they are really trying to control or deceive others. Flattery misused, and kind words not meant in kindness are lies with a loving aura. These words come from the dark place of fear. It's an empty soul that needs to pretend to love in order to be loved.

Spirituality: A Life Force

How desperately unworthy and alone we must feel when we think we have to bargain for, or buy love with our words, with our behaviors. We are all deserving of love without any conditions, without any reservations.

There's great power and great danger in words! Listen to them carefully knowing they're not always what they seem to be on the surface. Our words can be cloaked in false pride, manipulation, righteousness, and hidden anger. We can attempt to kill the loving spirit of another when we do not recognize our own loving spirit.

Words are spiritual tools and how we use them determines what we teach. Attacking words come from fear and generate more fear; love words come from love and generate more love. Grandiose words about our assets do not change the balance of power around us; these expressions do not make us more. They simply try to reduce others to a lesser place which doesn't exist. Less or more, right or wrong, are illusions. We are all one in God's Love!

As citizens of this world we need to be aware of the power of words--to bless others or to destroy their spirit. We teach what we are and we teach others what they are to us. As I said earlier, as a teacher in the classroom, I became aware of this power to change lives with positive approval, and loving encouraging words. I taught my subject but more importantly, I taught my students that I loved them. If I hadn't learned that early on and really believed and felt that, I would have failed and lost control of the class.

A powerful leader who doesn't have spiritual awareness himself cannot consider the spirit of others in delivering that power. A leader who is not spiritually aware can be addicted to upset and anger. Through reacting against this or that, they assert their feeling of self. A leader who's not spiritually aware strengthens his ego by always being "right". The narcissistic ego loves to make others wrong in order to get a stronger sense of who they are. Obviously, they are not operating as children of God who see all others as equal children of God. I believe, that any leader whether it's the parent, teacher, manager, president, prime minister, or anyone who has power over others, needs to consider the spiritual essence of those they lead. Cruel and hateful remarks, name calling, constant resentful and angry expressions damage souls leaving marks that can last a life time. I believe when a person of power damages anyone at a spiritual level it is evil and the worst misuse of power.

Six Attributes of Loving Words

Loving expression heals with patience, respect, sincerity, humility and generosity. These are the six attributes that come forth when we teach only love:

Patience: The first attribute is patience. Being patient in your words is an act of love. Listening to the message of others, and taking time to hear each word is the patience of love. Answering carefully and with deliberation is love. So many words are misunderstood because they are abruptly spoken. Being considerate of the feelings of others by being patient is an act of love.

Kindness: The second attribute is kindness. Using words that we would like to hear shows kindness in our verbal expression. We need to think of how our words are received. Are we gentle? Are we using endearments? Are we using words of love as we speak? Or are we bullying, berating, and badgering people with words? Words can be kind and gentle, or harsh and cruel. We are the messengers! Ask yourself, "What am I teaching?"

Respect: The third attribute is respect. What is the tone of your words? Are they respectful of the true role of the other person? Do we really respect their spirituality? Or do we discount them? Respect means equality--even if they are different, poor, handicapped, or even if they attack you with harsh resentful words. The respect we hold for others shows in the way we speak to them.

Sincerity: The fourth attribute of loving expression is sincerity. Without sincerity, words become lies. There's no way that a person can judge whether your words are coming from love or fear. You are the perpetrator of those words--you are the only one who knows what is inside you. When you operate out of fear, you will lie; but when you are a child of God, your fear will be gone and you will be able to love unconditionally. To teach only love is to respect the Godliness of the person to whom you communicate.

Once in a church meeting, I sat next to a man who moved me to great compassion. He was so thin and gaunt that it seemed as if his very bones would break out of his skin. His eyes were protruding from their sockets; his face grey and gaunt. After a long bout of disease, it was obvious that he was struggling, very near death, and--it would not be many days. His presence next to me filled me with the need to reach out to him and touch him.

Christine A. Adams

When the meeting was over, I stood up, hesitated, but knew I needed to speak to him. I turned to him and said, "God be with you" and asked if I could hug him. He stood up and allowed me to hug him. His frail body seemed all bones and no flesh. Then, he thanked me for touching him. I understood. Once again, I said "God be with you." I know he knew I sensed his fear, and his isolation, and I know he felt the sincerity of my words.

Humility: The fifth attribute to expressing loving words is humility. I might have avoided this man out of a sense of false pride. Would he think me foolish? Would he think I pitied him? Was I trying to be a "do-gooder"? There's humility in the expression of loving words because sometimes we have to remove ourselves, our egos, from the situation and get completely outside ourselves. Sometimes we have to be humble enough to do something uncommon, or even risk rejection. When we humble ourselves by risking, we love. When we speak directly from the heart, from the soul, we might seem out of place, but it will be done in love.

Generosity: The sixth attribute in loving expression is generosity. It takes selflessness to listen to the words of others and to take time to respond. It takes energy to communicate fairly and lovingly. How much easier it is to say, "You make me angry!" How simple it is to blame someone else. The real difficulty lies in the words, "I feel angry about this situation." How much more loving it is to claim the anger as yours and not accredit it to someone else. Loving words require a generosity, an "owning up" to the responsibility of our feelings, and a generous release of all around us from that responsibility.

Generosity in loving words takes energy, concentration and time. Rather than reacting immediately to some affront, we need to think the situation through--and stay with our own feelings. It takes time and energy to practice this type of response. Whenever you feel a surge of anger, let it be a warning bell that alerts your attention. Concentrate. Why are you feeling this way? What has happened in the relationship that produced that anger. Own it! Speak about it or it will fester. Before we can deal with any emotion, we need to understand it. The last thing we need to do is to transfer it to the closest person by saying "You made me angry!"

Generous loving expression is not a series of questions veiled in some hidden agenda. It is straightforward, not overt. It says, "I feel lonely today and I need you to stay with me for a few hours." Not, "What are you planning to do today?" Where are you going now?" "Where will you be this afternoon?" Generous loving expression does not set traps so that our partners fall into "saying the wrong thing", or "saying the right thing." Generous loving expression just is! It tells the truth, it does not look for answers and it does not omit important information.

It is said that God works through others. Not only does God use our actions, but He uses our words. We can be teachers and lovers, or we can destroy with attack and hatred. Sometimes words are so subtly spoken that they don't seem dangerous, but, in time, they will erode confidence and spirit.

Unsolicited criticism is attack because it's not specifically called for by the other person. There's no need to chance the damage of someone's spirit with well meaning "criticism."

Words and Children: Parents are the guardians of their child's delicate spirit; parents need to look carefully at the words they speak in frustration and anger. Words can destroy.

Especially vulnerable are little children. I cringe when I hear a mother say, "You're a bad boy." "You never do anything right." I die inside when I hear an older sister telling a younger child, "You can't do that."

Negative words cling like parasites and, eventually, corrupt the perception and performance of adults. You might think we would outgrow these words, and, in truth, we get older but in our subconscious minds they lurk waiting to crop up and haunt us. If we could dismiss damaging words, wash them away like dirt, we would never have to face them; but we can't. Words are so powerful because they become imbedded in our minds becoming part of our inner voice.

Then, as Ruth Fishel said in her work, **The Power of Words**, "We are moved by the messages we tell ourselves. They create positive or negative, healing or destructive actions and feelings. Our bodies respond to them with sickness or health."

My father, an uneducated immigrant from Ireland, was a proud, hardworking man who loved children. The words of praise he used were coveted by all eight of us, the "darlin's" and "dearies" that rolled off his Gaelic tongue were prized beyond measure. Like many of the Irish, he was a man of power when it came to words. My father loved to story-tell and gave a near reverence to the detail of any expression. It was a treat to be the subject of his story. However, if he was not proud of you, or if he could not bring himself to praise, the silence was deadly.

Every day we have an opportunity to touch children with our words of love, or we can choose to harm others with words that produce sickness. That's the challenge of using words as a healing force. To speak your love. To take the love from inside you and give it away to your children. We may give material gifts to those we love but these gifts will deteriorate with time losing their value, their newness, their fashion. But in the end, only words last forever.

The Writer and Words: Few know more about words than the writer. We have had a lifelong love affair with words and come to respect their power. We read, and read, and assimilate and digest words and; then, recast them giving them back to you in new messages. We embrace you or assail you through words.

Sometimes we are stripped of everything until there is nothing but the spoken word. In the following narrative using the fictional character name, Jenny, I have recounted such a time for me: a fictional rendition of the day my first husband, the father of my children, died of cancer. Several years before his sickness, we had gone through a bitter divorce that was not characterized by loving words. On the contrary, there had been years of fear and anger. However, in the time he had before his terminal cancer took his life, we had made peace and were able to communicate. Then, finally in the end, I was stripped of everything but my words. In a previous book, I recounted this fictional narrative of the last few moments of my first husband's life. I share this story with you now:

Route Two arched toward Concord, Mass. She remembered the rotary and the ominous prison buildings on the right. "My God", she said. "I remember the times we drove together by this place, over this road."

Trying to propel her rushed thoughts backwards to their college days, to the football games at Boston College, and to the visits to his parent's home, Jenny forgot for a moment the reason for her trip today. It had been an arrogant mother--in--law who never accepted Jenny, and a father--in--law who had. Then, seventeen years of marriage, three children and a bitter divorce due to alcoholism.

Jenny sighed as she checked the road signs. Concord never changes she thought with its typical old colonial houses, painted white with black shutters, stately, hard to heat, with the widow's walks on the roof. But this day was not for sightseeing.

"Some place it should say Cameron Hospital", she said aloud. Then Jenny saw the sign with a big H on it and turned right. Another right and into the parking garage. She took a ticket and circled several times before finding an empty space. Anxious and frustrated, she walked briskly towards the gate keeper. Agitated, she muttered, "I can't imagine having to pay to go see someone in the hospital--maybe even die." The young attendant just shrugged her shoulders.

Once inside, Jenny impatiently waited as the elevator descended. She tried to put the years together--their marriage ended fifteen years ago, nine more years of alcoholism, sobriety and recovery; and then four years of diabetes and cancer and now, and his imminent death.

But they said the cancer was in his brain she thought. How long can it be if that is true? She answered her own question by thinking that no one ever knows. Then, gratitude for the last

Spirituality: A Life Force

four years of wonderful moments, for reconciliation, for the peace they had come to as a couple, as a family.

When Jenny walked into the room, she moved quickly to his bedside. Something was terribly wrong. This was different! She knew immediately that he was dying! Her first thought was the children. Then she moved closer to the man who had given her those children, who had been her husband. As she held his hand, his whole body shook in the throes of death. It was as if his spirit was fighting to be released from his body--every spasmodic movement of his deteriorated body brought death one second closer. There was no time!!

"Someone call the children," she said to those standing by.

"Tell them there is no time."

"Quickly", she said in a hushed voice so that he would not hear. Jenny remembered how her daughter had promised her father that she would be with him at the end. She knew she was driving there at this moment.

She remembered the concern in her oldest son's voice when he said he would take the next flight. There was no time! She remembered the preoccupation of her youngest son just hours before as he hesitantly went to work. Above all, she knew that he loved his children more than anything in the world and that they loved him. Then again, to anyone who would listen, "Hurry, try to contact the children."

In the hall was his estranged brother, his only brother, whom he believed had disrespected him his whole life. He had begged his family not to allow this brother near him when he was dying. There was no comfort there.

Back at his bedside, she held his hand and comforted him with her words. "It is alright." she said. "You are alright." More wracking moments of pain; they were rhythmic, never ceasing. More words.

"The children are coming. They love you." He tried to speak but could not form the words from a parched mouth. Afraid to witness his dying moments or to be with him, the brother and his family hung back in fear as they watched from the hall. Despite their watchful eyes, she continued on.

"I understand." she whispered. and finally, "I love you." These were words familiar to him but not expressed by her since the days of their marriage. He tried to respond but could not.

She said again, "I know. I understand."

Miraculously, in a few moments their youngest son would get to his bedside simply by "thinking something was wrong and rushing over to the hospital." It was minutes before his death. In the end, the wracking movements of pain stopped as his skin turned jaundiced yellow, and blood trickled from his mouth. The usefulness of his body was over as his spirit left his body. At that moment, his son touched his father's head and said, "Peace, Dad, Peace."

Jenny leaned in closer and whispered, "You can go now. It's OK. I will take care of the children. God will take you home. We will follow you!" At that moment she saw an imprint of what had been his physical form slowly rise upwards. He was gone.

Spirituality: A Life Force

On those words, it was over. In that instant, words were the last gift to be given to a dying loved one. They were the only gift that could be given.

Every day we have an opportunity to touch others with our words of love, or we can choose to harm others with words that produce fear and hatred. That is the challenge of living-in-love--to speak it! To take the love from inside and give it away to others. We may give material gifts to those we love but these gifts will deteriorate with time losing their value, their newness, their fashion. But in the end, only words last forever.

The Healing Power of Forgiveness

Without ***A Course In Miracles***, I couldn't have internalized the concept of forgiveness as a primary function in my life. I had to understand that there was no other choice for me to gain freedom and to understand that true forgiveness would benefit me! Through a real and genuine forgiveness of myself and others, I came to know real peace. Therefore forgiveness became a tool for healing.

A Course In Miracles states that: "Those who forgive are releasing themselves from the illusion, while those who withhold forgiveness are binding themselves to illusion." The illusion is that we are separate entities, not children of God sharing a common salvation. The illusion is that if we forgive, we will be condoning someone else's sins. The illusion tells us that if we declare someone else sinless in the eyes of God that we'll be less. It says, "They might be right and we might be wrong!" The reality is that we are all one, all perfect in the sight of God. It's our primary function to forgive, to change our perception and see others as God's children.

Author of ***Love Is Letting Go of Fear***, Gerald Jamplosky puts it this way, "Forgiveness is the vehicle used for correcting our misconceptions, and for helping us to let go of fear. Simply stated, to forgive is to let go." By letting go, we surrender and turn to God for the help finally understanding how powerless we are. Then, God becomes the solution!

Thoughts of God replace obsessive thoughts, and there's freedom--a release from all that has robbed us of freedom. With any obsession there is an attempt to fill a spiritual void. It's an inner gnawing that never gets better no matter what you do! It always returns to plague you. Once it's filled with love, that love will extend itself out to others in forgiveness. Our primary function is a loving one-- forgiveness.

At first it takes enormous concentration and courage to let go of obsessions, but that's the only way to freedom and peace. Trying to control anything except my own spiritual growth is futile. Simply put, it means "tend to your own business." And, the business of a child of God is love!!

Love is what you are, love is what you do--love does not resent, hate, or attack--it forgives! Forgiveness is the function of love. In order for me to be true to what I am, I must make a decision to forgive myself, first; and then, others. Love forgives all. There's no picking and choosing even when we feel gravely wronged.

All of us are joined to God through His Love. Being at One with others is the only logical way if we view God as Love.

God does not judge or exclude: therefore, we're asked not to judge or exclude. That does not mean I have to condone anyone's behavior, accept abuse, or even agree with someone, but I must forgive. In order to be free, I must let others go! It was once said, "To forgive is to set a prisoner free and discover that prisoner was me."

Forgiveness is not forgetting. We learn not to be victimized for two reasons: to never let it happen again and to avoid victimizing others. If we forget, we will repeat that situation again with different players in a different scene. Neither is forgiving a form of self-sacrifice or a pretense of being good. Once again that positioning comes from ego-based thinking that puts me above you. Forgiveness is a gift to me! It's a clear cut decision to enter a process of healing. It's a decision to let go of anger, resentment, ego, self-pity, and personal hurt. It may take time but it's a gift to the self that is worth waiting for. Let no one stand in the way of your gift to you!

But, you might say I can't forgive this person, or that one particular incident. It's impossible to let it go. Forgiveness is a primary function of love! It's a healing process--but we must be willing to heal.

If a sore is left to fester it will get worse, or better in a random way, but if a wound is tended to, it should heal. So it is with any damage inflicted on us. Pope Paul knew the power of defenselessness when he went to speak with the man who attempted to kill him. It seemed he knew that this face-to-face meeting would bring healing. It seemed he choose not to stay in a victim role. By becoming the perpetrator of forgiveness, of love and of peace, he accomplished his own spiritual healing.

To hang onto resentment is to harbor a thief in the heart. By the minute and the hour, resentment steals joy we could treasure now and remember forever. It pilfers our energy to celebrate life--to face others as messengers of grace rather than ambassadors of doom. We victimize ourselves when we withhold forgiveness.

Perhaps we are making excuses for our inability to live--in--love. Forgiving implies hard work, it involves process. Watch a physical wound heal. It changes day by day needing different treatments at different stages of recovery. So it is with forgiveness. Any healing process will take different forms depending on the nature of the hurt and the depth of the wound. Here are some steps you might encounter. They might not appear exactly in this order as each person processes differently. Also, there are times when you might back track and become re-infected with the sickness that brought on the hurt.

Denial: In this early stage, we might deny the intensity of the hurt and down play our feelings about the situation. However, the hurt is there and will resurface to get our attention.

Self-blame: There's a tendency to be judgmental in the second stage. How could I have been so stupid to trust that person? Why did I accept a situation at face value? Sometimes in hindsight, we can see how thing might have been different if only we knew what we know now.

Victim: The second and third stages blend into a victim attitude. We might wallow in self-pity at this point and let ourselves become less disciplined because we are sorry for ourselves.

Anger: Eventually anger will set in and we will get mad at the person who hurt us or perhaps at the world or even worse at God. We will become less tolerant and more self-righteous.

Self-forgiveness: At this point, we begin to see that the situation taught us some valuable lessons which we might not have learned another way. Perhaps it takes a similar situation which we handle in a different way to remind us of what we have learned. Then, we are grateful for the lesson. We survive, and go on knowing we did the best we could with the knowledge we had at the time.

Forgiveness of others: We acknowledge that the person who hurt us did the best they could at that time. We recognize that although we don't condone their behavior--they are also children of God and need to be viewed as more than their negative behaviors. We can let go by releasing the energy we were using to blame them and ourselves. When we release this energy, we can go on to a healthy, unencumbered and peaceful state.

The path of healing through forgiveness is not a straight line as the stages of healing are never linear. We slip and slide, back and forth, in an out of denial, anger and awareness. Be patient with yourself and be assured that if you work at it consistently and willingly, you will be healed. You are a child of God, you are perfect just the way you are--today!!

The Healing Power of Prayer and Meditation

During the day, there's no special time for prayer and meditation. If you "seek" to pray, you will find time during the day to make conscious contact with God. Any moment can become a prayerful moment. Here are some kinds of daily prayers:

Prayers of Praise: There are holy moments all day long. During those moments we can thank God for His beneficence. It can be as simple as seeing a child, having your car start, or being able to successfully finish as important task. Whenever two people share a loving moment--that is prayer. Whenever someone forgives--that is prayer. Whenever anyone makes a decision to stay away from a harmful situation--that is prayer. Whenever people meet and share their experience, strength and hope--that is prayer.

Prayers of praise are the fillers of my day as I observe all the things in my life I wish to thank God for. They come in a flash of appreciative contact with God.

Prayers of Petition: There are many people and situations in our lives that are beyond our control. Petitioning God to deal with those people and situations is a prayer of petition. Whether it's a critically sick friend, or a bothersome neighbor, we don't always have to carry the burden of worry, or annoyance, that goes along with life. We can do what's possible and necessary and then turn those people and situations over to the care of God.

It's self-defeating to become overpowered by anger and resentment. The best I can do is release it and pray that God take care of that person or situation. Prayers of petition can free us from the people and situations in our life over which we have no control.

Spirituality: A Life Force

Prayers of Acceptance: We "pray only for the knowledge of His Will". I believe that frequent prayers of praise and petition during the day help us to learn the knowledge of God's Will. When we look at the world with praise and gratitude, we are more likely to see the many gifts God gives us. When we see these gifts, we accept the good in our life. I believe "God's will for me is joy." I need only see it. Acceptance always brings joy.

When we are able "to turn our life and will over to the care of God as we understand Him", we begin to accept some of the things we do not yet understand. Prayers for acceptance are closely tied to our petitions for God's help with people, places and things in our life--because by admitting I am powerless over those things, I accept that God is in control. I succumb to His plan even when I don't understand the outcome. I simply believe, without fear, that "all things work together for good for those who love God. " Romans 8:28

Prayers for Power: There's no greater power than God. I must turn to Him whenever I need the power to go on with my life. Faith dispels fear and prayer increases faith. So, whenever there is the overwhelming presence of fear, prayers for power will help. Having a mantra, or short prayer, in mind when we need to reach for God's help is really beneficial. Here are the mantras I rely on: "God is the love in which live. and "The strength of God in me is successful in all things." Both are taken from *A Course In Miracles*. I use the Serenity prayer as well: "God grant me the Serenity to accept the things I cannot change; The Courage to change the things I can, and Wisdom to know the difference." (Reinhold Neibuhr)

After we acknowledge that God is the primary force in our lives, we reach out through prayer, reading, and meditation. In **Spirituality and Recovery,** Father Leo Booth says: "Meditation is a technique of realizing our full potential as human beings and living our lives to the fullest. It is about finding time and discovering the time "to be". It is placing the physical, mental, and emotional aspects of our lives in an at-one-ment. It is using silence to say yes."

There're no set patterns for meditation since it's primarily experiential. It's being still and knowing God. It's being still and being grateful to God. It's concentrating on the word "peace" or "love" until we internalize it. It may be reading special words meditatively. It may be different for each person but for all it awakens the spark of the Divine within us.

Spiritual healing can happen in relationships, in a family structure, in society itself through words, forgiveness, and prayer and meditation. We do what we can by watching our words, by making forgiveness our primary function and by seeking the help of God through prayer and meditation. When spiritual healing happens it becomes a spiritual event: a miracle.

Chapter 8

Spiritual Solutions

We all struggle to find solutions to our problems. Some problems seem bigger than others, some we can handle. We look at others who have more difficulty and wonder how we would deal with such huge problems. Sometimes we even feel fortunate not to have their problems; other times small problems get exaggerated in our minds. A unsightly cold sore is smaller than cancer: bankruptcy is larger than not being able to pay this month's electric bill. However, both are problems!

In Wayne Dyer's book, **There's *A Spiritual Solution To Every Problem***, he explains that spirit, the formless, invisible energy which is the sustenance of life on this planet--and the life of God within us--can solve every problem that we encounter. Our life force of spirit has a purpose!

Basically, spiritual solutions are only a thought or two away. In our materially oriented world, we have many problems--even ones that seem insoluble. A shift in thinking is required in order to discover that we have something at our disposal: something we can use every time we face a problem. We need to see ourselves containing a force that can be called upon for spiritual solutions.

In chapter three I discussed spiritual identity--or seeing myself as a child of God. To me, false identification with the material world, the ego-based world, led me to a basic misunderstanding of my real nature. In that chapter, I detailed my spiritual journey to a new spiritual identity. Actually, the journey did not consist of my arriving at a new destination where I gained this new identity but rather consisted of the dissipation of my ignorance concerning myself and life itself.

Then came the gradual growth of that understanding which began as a spiritual awakening. The finding of God became my coming to my Self. The finding of the God within me, knowing I am a child of God, helped me see that I myself contain a spiritual force that is available for solutions to any problem. All I needed to do was access that spiritual force.

As Marianne Williamson states in her latest book, ***Tears to Triumph*** published in 2016, "Everyone is on a spiritual journey; most people just don't know it. Spirituality refers not to some theological dynamic outside ourselves, but to how we choose to use our minds. The spiritual path is the path of the heart; at every moment, we're walking the path of love and creating happiness or swerving from it and creating suffering. Every thought we think leads deeper into love or deeper into fear".

Once I discovered my spiritual identity, I began to live a different life. In chapter Four, I explained how my awareness changed once I internalized my spiritual identity by "knowing" who I really am--a child of God. Then, relationships with others changed as I changed. Now I could see others as children of God as well. Finally, I was capable of entering "holy relationships" as defined in Chapter five and six. The entire paradigm of my life shifted as all relationships took on spiritual purposes.

Spirituality: A Life Force

As Marianne Williamson goes on to say in **Tears to Triumph,** *"The spiritual universe is the Mind of God. Miracles are thoughts of love, extended from the mind of God through the mind of humans and out into the world. God is Love, and as God's children, so are we. Our purpose on earth is to think as God thinks, which means to love as God loves. When our minds are attuned to love, things unfold miraculously. Loving thoughts create loving feelings, and loving feelings create loving behavior. In this way we create happiness for ourselves and those around us."*

As a result of this spiritual shift, explained in earlier chapters, I began to experience healing in my life--through words, forgiveness, and prayer. Finally, I discovered that my new found spiritual awareness lead me to spiritual solutions for everyday problems. Thus, these final chapter explains that process as well as the rewards of "all things spiritual."--and the possibly of miracles.

SPIRITUAL SOLUTIONS

Where do we start? Quietly communing with God, when we are searching for guidance, we turn to God as a way of temporarily turning off our ego-mind. Instead of our ego-self thinking, "I can fix this," we become willing to immerse our thoughts into our higher self. With our divine connection, we are always in touch with the solution. In times of crisis and strife, it's time to "Let go and Let God". When you can do that, you move to a place of peace.

SURRENDER

Many people feel that they must do something to take care of their problems. Most of the time that's true. I'm not suggesting that you simply abandon your responsibilities and turn everything over to God. If you don't work, you can't pay the bills, if you don't take care of your health, you will be sick. I believe it's our duty to "do the next right thing"; but, when we encounter something that's out of our hands to fix, we need to surrender to God.

The inner dialogue might go something like this:"I don't know how to fix this problem and I've done all that I can do. Now, I'm turning it over to the same force that I turn my body over to every night when I sleep. I trust that force to keep my heart beating and my lungs breathing. This force, that may be called God, is always available, an invisible force that is my strength." Sometimes I simply repeat my mantra, "the strength of God in me is successful in all things". That doesn't mean some things, but, all things--even the latest problem that is bothering me.

RETURN TO LOVE AND FORGIVENESS

Activating spiritual solutions means converting inner thoughts and feelings from anxiety, worry and disharmony to love. God is Love. So, when I can substitute Love for anguish and frustration, I am immediately empowered. When I am plugged into inner thoughts that are connected to the material world, I feel upset, hurt, and even hopeless in terms of being able to solve or correct any problem. Defining my power only in material world terms is really a reflection of being spiritually disconnected.

RECOGNIZING THE INFINITE

Carl Yung reminds us that "the telling question of a person's life is their relationship to the Infinite." If I accept that all life is indestructible in the sense that our spirit is inseparable from the Infinite, it puts things in perspective for me.

Sometimes I have to remind myself that I am not God; therefore, I do not know what is the best outcome is in this situation. There are so many things my finite mind cannot understand. Why would I be able to predict the solution to this problem?

In order to get back to a place of peace and contentment, I need to be quiet, empty my mind and let go of my ideas about exactly how something should be resolved. In silent meditation, I can listen and allow my mind to be still becoming open to what will inevitable come to me. One of my favorite biblical quotes is, "Be still and Know that I am God." Psalms 46:10

There's no room for hanging onto "who did what and when" and "how wrong they were." It's a time for forgiveness. As I stated in a previous chapter, forgiveness becomes a gift to me freeing me from pent up resentments, hatred and revenge. A place of forgiveness is a better mind-set for problem resolution.

AN ATTITUDE OF GRATITUDE

For me, one of the key ingredients to finding my way out of a negative space is to be grateful. There's always something to be grateful for. When you're grateful, your mind shifts to a positive place forcing you out of the negative energy that comes when you're overcome by worry. Seek that positive thing to be grateful for and bring it up in your mind throughout the day. Remember to remember it when dark thoughts emerge.

Recently, I was worried about a grandchild who suddenly developed mononucleosis during his high school senior year--a crucial time. He was being evaluated by college coaches for a soccer scholarship; his grades were being submitted for college entrance. Now, he was unable to play soccer, or even get to school. The timing of his sickness couldn't have been worse. Ironically, during that same time period, my best friend's grandson was killed in an automobile accident. Knowing how she was grieving the permanent loss of someone she loved put my worry and concern in perspective. So, I turned my grandson over to God and stopped worrying knowing that whatever solution presented itself; it would be the right one. Ironically, the transformation within him during that time of sickness made him a stronger adult.

I am grateful to all the "spiritual teachers" who have taught the lessons of this book. To my family members for their love and patience with me over the years--my children, husband, grand children, step children, editors, publishers, teachers, students, authors, sponsors, and mentors. And to you, reader, I am grateful that I made this journey so that I could share it with you! I am grateful that you were there with me.

Spirituality: A Life Force

You are seekers. Just like me! You might be in recovery, or therapy, looking for spiritual answers. You might be anyone, of any age, who is looking for serenity through a spiritual transformation, or a spiritual awakening. You may simply be seeking for more answers to a meaningful life path. You are a thinker who goes beyond the surface of our concrete physical selves-and is open to the possibility of the spiritual self. God allowed me to learn from all of you about making "spirituality" the vital force in my life. Thank you!

LOVE AND FEAR

Generally, there are two overriding emotions--love and fear. These emotions cannot be experienced simultaneously. If I have fear, I have eliminated love, and vice versa. The Bible tells us, "God is Love, and he who abides in love abides in God, and God in him." (1 John4:16). So obviously the solution is to rid myself of fear by stopping myself in a moment of fear and replacing that fear with my faith in God. If I allow the presence of God, to slip into that place where fear had resided, I can go on.

In my fearful concern for the future of my grandchild, I was playing God. I had a pattern of perfection set up for his last year of high school. After all he had worked for many years to accomplish these goals. I feared his college career would be gone, he would be left struggling in the future. The opposite happened when his sickness gave him a renewed strength and appreciation for life and he played for four years Santa Clara University--a California Division One College. Last year he completed his third year as a professional soccer player in both Finland and Iceland.

THE TRUE NATURE OF PROBLEMS

The problems we experience are really illusions of the material world. What if this happens or that doesn't? What if God is punishing me because I sinned? Sometimes these are harmful guilt ridden thoughts. These are the thoughts that separate us from God who is always the solution. Our only problem is separation from God--from Love--which is our most natural state of being, the state that brings harmony and serenity.

GETTING OFF TRACK SPIRITUALLY

Very few people can say that they never get off track and get lost in problems of the world. Very few people can say they're in harmony with their spirit at all times. But we can prudently observe ourselves as we live our lives as we act and react. By noticing we are off track spiritually we can redirect our energy back to God. **Here are seven negative patterns that seem to reoccur with me:**

First, I lose my spiritual identification! When the world begins to consume me with schedule, responsibilities, and simple physical survival, I can lose sight of my Infinite spiritual nature. I can forget to say to myself, "I am a child of God. I am protected. I am cared for." For me, I need to remind myself with these positive affirmations. Daily prayer and meditation help because they reinforce my spiritual identification.

Second, I become fearful without spiritual support. Once the fear is allowed into my mind, it eases out the loving support of God. Fear is like a sickness: it grows and spreads taking on a life of its own. Of myself, I am weak and fearful but with God within me, I am powerful and unafraid.

Third, once the fear takes hold I become spiritually disconnected and governed by that fear. Here is when the worry and obsession starts and my ego tries to find ways to fix the problem. Forgetting I am ill-equipped to handle most problems, I become anxious and agitated.

Fourth, I hang onto the problem because there doesn't seem to be a solution. I forget to turn it over to God and stubbornly refuse to recognize my own limited, finite understanding as I try to play God. As long as I am in this state, there is discontent and agitation.

Fifth, I let in all kinds of judgments. Judgments are those negative thoughts of blaming. If only they had done this or that, the problem would not exist. Why can't they change or see the way of their errors? Round and round it goes! As it develops I become enamored with the problem and it seems to become a part of my everyday life.

Sixth, with all of this negative thinking, I construct a barrier to my connection with my spiritual self. Here's where I begin to see myself as a victim, or not worthy, or as guilty, or as sinful--but not a spiritual child of God.

Seventh, in this negative state I forget, or refuse to make conscious contact with God. By not doing so, I go deeper into the problem, into the ego based material world. By not slowing down to reach out to God in prayer and meditation, I perpetuate the problem and deny myself the spiritual solution.

There's a spiritual solution to every problem! The only problem I ever have is my separation from God--from Love, or basically from myself. Being able to understand the downward spiral and being able to interrupt it can bring me back to a place of peace, where I can reach out to God in prayer and meditation and find that spiritual solution.

So, as you face a problem, remind yourself you created it with one mind, and you can solve it with another mind-set. Our problems came from a negative place--but a spiritual solution is readily available if we create positive energy to access it.

In the writing of this book, this very chapter, I took time off to spiral out of control right into a problem. Then when I came back to what I had written here, my mind-set changed. Just knowing it's possible to change negative thoughts to a positive spiritual energy was reassuring--a relief. Now I am back on the right track to a peaceful place. I wrote the following Care Note during this time:

When You're Facing A Difficult Time: 7 Spiritual Steps

By Christine A Adams

Whether it's health crisis, family tragedy, or sudden death of a loved one, there are times when life is more difficult than others. Life is a vicarious experience-- always changing, always full of unpredictable situations. Some events bring great joy and happiness and others danger, difficulty and even turmoil. There are no guarantees that these difficult times won't come to all of us.

Working Your Way through

Over my lifetime, I have faced challenges: I lost a parent when I was a child, lost a child as a parent, faced tragedy, poverty, addiction, divorce, bankruptcy and several major surgeries. These situations, which demanded faith, courage, gratitude, and finally acceptance, provided me my greatest spiritual lessons. But you might ask what can I do? Here are seven steps to take when your life shifts into a difficult time.

Step One: Recognize The Fear

Difficult situations usually cause fear. When we rely on our own power, we're afraid. We think we have to handle the situation with our human powers; yet, we know the difficulty is so powerful it could overwhelm us. When fear goes unchecked, it can accelerate until it does overcome us. Over the years, I've learned that the only antidote to such a fearful state is faith. When I turn to God, I remember there is nothing to fear.

Step Two: Remember God's Strength

Whenever you're afraid, it's a sure sign you're trusting in your own strength. Think about this: what is there in your previous experience that proves you can control any situation? How can you be aware of all the facets of any situation? How can you, alone, resolve a problem in such a way that only good will come from it? What can you control?

By yourself, you can't control the actions and decisions of others, especially those people who aren't close to you, or even those who are closest to you. You can't control certain random situations that cause irreversible damage. Some tragic events seem senseless and unfair. Most things in life are random and full of mystery. The only thing you can control is yourself and your reaction to life as it unfolds for you.

To believe you can control the outcome of anything is putting your trust where trust is unwarranted. It may lead to fear, anxiety, or depression. How can you feel safe if you put your faith in human frailties? Again for me, the only antidote is faith. God is the strength in which I trust. God is my safety in all circumstances.

When I remind myself of these things, I remember God. Then I know there is nothing to fear!

Step Three: Let Go and Let God

Once you have remembered God and begun to rely on His strength, you have to let go of the outcome of the difficulty. That doesn't mean you don't do all "the next right things". You do! If you need medical help from a doctor, you seek one out. If you need legal help, you go to a lawyer. If you need to seek counsel from professionals, friends, or family, you go to them. And listen carefully praying for guidance.

Letting go to God does not mean that we have an excuse to stop fighting through to a solution to this difficult problem. It doesn't mean that we rationalize deciding that we don't have to take any action in this situation. It doesn't mean God will do all the work while we take it easy. Or that we read God's will into every vicarious happening around us. It means that we will do all that we can but the outcome is in God's hands.

Step Four: Find Gratitude in Any situation

Having gratitude for what we have and for what we can do helps us appreciate what God is doing for us. In grieving the loss of a loved one, we can claim small victories with gratitude. Years ago, when my child died a few days after birth, I found a young mother who had lost twins. She lifted me from my solitary sorrow because her loss was double. Recently, when my sister died, I missed her terribly but I was extremely grateful for the years we had together. I believe **God is always providing us something to be grateful for if we look for it. In difficult times, finding gratitude is a precious gift that brings us closer to acceptance of "what is."**

The ability to relax and be mindfully present in the moment comes naturally when you're grateful. Gratitude thoughts are positive, healthy thoughts. Listen to what you're thinking, feeling and saying. When you're thinking positive thoughts your body and spirit remain strong and healthy. Amazingly, these thoughts will bring more things to be grateful for.

Be grateful for the journey of life--the joyful moments and the difficulties. When you're tempted to put more energy into the obstacles and diversions on your path than on your mission, remember to be grateful for what these difficult times teach; but go on with courage.

Step Five: Find Courage through Acceptance

Courage is simply a matter of acceptance of the things you can't change and then being willing to change the things you can. Courage is simply doing "the next right thing" and not getting lost in trying to change "what Is." It means going on when things are difficult and maintaining a sense of hope rather than one of despair, regrets, or self-pity. Sometimes it means total reliance on God to find the wisdom to know what to do, what to say, or how to act. We are all looking for "the next right thing?"

But what if a terrible tragedy happens?

I don't believe it's God's will when tragedy strikes: a loved one is killed, or a loved one is diagnosed with a cancer, or has a drug or alcohol addiction. Life is full of vagaries--switches and changes. Blaming God for misfortune is a dangerous place to be. This idea puts us in touch with a judgmental, punitive God, not a loving God.

Spirituality: A Life Force

I believe "I am a child of God" with a physical self that is mortal, or temporary, and a spiritual self that is immortal, or permanent. It's the spiritual side that makes me related to God, a God of love. I believe that God loves me and, like any parent of any child, that "God's will for me is joy."

All we have to do is accept the vagaries of life and be happy. Because we have free will, we can make our own mental state; we can choose to be full of joy and glad to be alive, or unhappy, resentful or bitter. A victim! For me, when I choose to remember my spiritual self, to remember God and accept His love, I can be happy. Not a victim but victorious!

Step Six: Connect to God through Prayer and Meditation

A natural flow of energy comes and goes in the physical world. Birth and death are part of that flow. Look to all things in nature and you will witness this truth. It's the spiritual that is constant and unchanging. We can stay connected to the spiritual, to God, through prayer and meditation. For me, to be out of touch with God seems like a place of "spiritual darkness." Every day I pray for God's guidance for the wisdom to know what I can change and what I can't. Every day I pray for gratitude, acceptance and moments of joy.

When faced with a difficult time, we can turn to God because there's no greater power than God. We need that power now. Faith in God dispels fear and prayer and meditation increase faith. So, when you're afraid, prayers for power help. When you think about it, no matter what a day brings, there's an unending source of power to draw on through prayer. All you need to do is reach out to connect and reconnect--with God's power! You can do that by spiritual readings or with repeated mantras like: "God is the love in which I live" or "The strength of God in me is successful in all things."

When faced with a difficult time, you can be grateful to have God as your guide. The strength of God in you is successful in all things-- not some things but all things. God is your safety in all circumstances – not some circumstances but all circumstances. His voice speaks to you for Him in all situations, telling you exactly what to do as you call upon His strength and protection. You can make it through these difficulties when you live in the appreciation of the endless love of God. So many times in my life I have felt the power of God getting me through a difficulty.

Step Seven: Live One Day at a Time

When thoughts of the past, or fear of the future, crowd into your mind, remember this is the only day you have. The only day to endure, to live and to love. By living one day at a time, you can give your full attention to "doing the next right thing." By paying attention to this moment, you can remember there is nothing to fear. God is in charge of this moment and all you need do is let go and let God--for just this moment.

By being present in this moment, you can be aware of the miracles that are happening. You can see the things to be grateful for, even the things that seem to be reversals. These reversals can teach you to have patience and give you the momentum to move forward.

Spirituality: A Life Force

Take Heart

During this day, when you feel like you don't have the power to go on, you can pray for that power. You can pray for the power to endure any given moment. You can ask for guidance to accept any situation that is out of your control. There's nothing more powerful than God's love. You are His child and He loves you. When others can't help you, God is always there for you. You can always reach out for God in these difficult times.

Chapter 9

Spiritual Energy and Miracles

*I*n the book, **There's A Spiritual Solution To Every Problem** Wayne Dyer describes three distinct energy fields that we can enter. Dyer explains that ordinary human awareness and energy varies by degrees of "speed", or energy fields with different "frequencies'. He claims we have the ability to increase our frequency and enhance our energy field. By increasing the speed at which we vibrate, we move into the frequencies of the spirit and away from those grounded in the material world of problems. By choosing to eliminate whatever interferes with our increasing our highest energy levels and negotiating the presence of positive factors in our life, we can bring about spiritual solutions.

In the slowest vibrations we have illness and disharmony. In a faster field but still somewhat slow, we have an ordinary human awareness and finally; in the fastest field there is thought and spirit. In the faster vibration frequencies, we are able to invoke intuition, insight and other potential spiritual gifts that are dormant while we are in ordinary human awareness. I believe this higher level of energy is visible in those we might deem spiritual teachers.

The slowest level might be called ego-consciousness. At this frequency, we feel separate from everyone else and from the spiritual self. We are absorbed with self-importance defining ourselves by whatever we have and do--and what others think of us. Another level of energy, of ordinary human awareness, might be called "group consciousness" Here we identify ourselves on the basis of what groups we have chosen to align ourselves with or have been assigned by birthplace, ethnic identity, or cultural label. We are white, we are old, we are Chinese or we are Muslim. Although group consciousness is normal, this is a frequency where conflict resolution is accomplished by determining who is right, who is stronger, or more powerful. Feuds and wars can be the result of group consciousness. This competition causes disruption and sometimes destroys peace.

The final, highest frequency is "God Consciousness" where separation is unknown. In this state, we see no divisions and know we are connected to all living creatures. Problems evaporate when we know there are no accidents and process each event of our life from that prospective.

Getting to this higher frequency of God consciousness is not an ordinary occurrence. Those who do are blessed and their presence in our world blesses others. Some examples come to mind like Thich Nhat Hanh's teachings exemplified in his book ***Peace In Every Step***. We can't all reach this level of spiritual energy but we can recognize it in others.

Bob and I are have been blessed to know Nancy Stevenson, a woman who was able to reach these higher levels of spiritual energy. Her body was riddled with cancer so she endured radical surgery. Coming out of it, she would not use words of hopelessness, or despair but simply stated "There is only God."

Spirituality: A Life Force

She went through several surgeries to reconstruct her internal organs and at one point she was even declared "cancer free"; however, the disease always returned. Through all this struggle, she continued to be joyful, to reach out to help others, to remind others of the spiritual saying that "There is only God".

She believed she was healthy in the "spirit", living close to God even as her body deteriorated. It was palpable, her spiritual energy, and it grew as she came closer to death. Because this energy radiated from her, it touched and blessed us. There was no mistaking it!

Energy impacts us at all times and the frequency at which that energy moves determines our physical, mental and spiritual health. Albert Einstein once said, "Nothing happens until something moves." To create spiritual solutions, we must at least tentatively accept the idea of energy vibrations which we have the ability to raise to a higher level. If you are a child of God, you have the ability to access divine energy. Human energy is low, divine energy is without limit. Simple prayer is a signal sent between your mind and the universal mind of God. It's your attempt to get to a higher frequency.

NEGATIVE THINKING

Negative thoughts lower your energy frequency. Whenever I get caught in a negative place, more negative things seem to happen. When enough negative incidents occur, I realize I am producing my own negative environment operating in this lower energy frequency. It's almost as if I'm inviting trouble into my life. I can't explain this phenomena but bad things happen, one right after another, until I turn these thoughts into thoughts of gratitude, into prayers of thanksgiving, into a conscious contact with God. Then, it stops. As soon as I shift back to the positive, I attract positive things. Negative thoughts equal negative happenings: positive thoughts equal positive happenings. It's amazing.

The first thing I do when I start to spin down into a negative spiral is to stop and look for something to be grateful for. It could be the return to health after having an infection, the resolution of a serious problem within my family, the concerns for a child or grandchild. Whatever problem I worried about last--the one that has now evaporated--becomes the focus of my gratitude. When I focus on that positive resolution, all the minor grievances of today disappear.

POSITIVE THINKING

Positive thoughts are spiritual thoughts that lead to a higher spiritual energy, to serenity, to our natural state. It's important to remember that "as you think so shall you be". Once we understand that what we think about expands, we start to get more careful about what we think about. What happens is our positive thoughts radiate outwards to create positive circumstances in our lives. Here are some things to remember:

Remember to eliminate the lower negative energy fields which are fear, anger, resentment, shame, frustration, guilt, hatred, and general discontent. These thoughts interfere with reaching a more spiritual place. But it doesn't stop there. Removing the negative thoughts means filling the space with faster higher frequencies or positive thoughts.

Remember to bring in the positives which are love, surrender, gratitude, quiet connection with God, and cheerfulness. There's no longer room left for the negative. You do have a choice. You can eliminate negative thoughts. Watch your thinking!

Remember that all things pass. What you were concerned about last week has been resolved or changed to a new situation. Everything in the material world of form is in a constant state of change. But there's also the world of the changeless that we call God and it is this unchanging spirit that will transform or solve our problems.

Remember you just might not always know what is best. Sometimes we dismiss implausible spiritual answers that don't correspond to the way we decide our life should be structured. Turn it over to God.

ACHIEVING A POSITIVE GOAL

So does that mean we just throw our hands up and never try to achieve a positive goal? Absolutely not! They say, "God does the work but bring a shovel." We should always be focused on achieving some positive goal and become open to the possibility that it might turn out better than we planned. Here are four qualities needed to reach a positive goal:

1. DESIRE: First, we need to express what positive achievement we wish to accomplish. I want to publish a book can be an expressed desire. That's the start!

2. ASKING: Second, we need to become willing to ask God to guide us to a solution. The act of asking is a form of letting go.

3. INTENTION: Third, we take full responsibility for the commitment of our desire. There's no doubt that we can reach this goal; so, with complete dedication and supreme confidence we move toward our desire.

4. PASSION: Finally, there's a hardening of the will that helps us persist when outside forces might attempt to dissuade us from our desire. It all boils down to a simple idea that what you really, really, really, really, want you will usually get.

So, if you really want something, state your desire, ask God to guide you, be resolute in your will and move with passion towards your goal.

For thirty two years, I taught high school seniors. Sometimes kids can be confused about what they want and what they 'think' everyone else wants for them. So, each year I had them write down their desire on a tiny piece of paper and carry that paper with them in their wallet. They would write, "I want to be a teacher" "I want to be a doctor." "I want to fall in love and get married." Amazingly, as the years went by, the students came back to tell me that their wish came true. I became a believer. So, I began writing down all my heartfelt wishes: "I want to publish a book." "I want to return to health after surgery." "I want to marry a good man." When each thing came true, I removed it from my wallet. Today I still have some new slips of paper in my wallet. They still come true. Try it!

The Law of Attraction

So what's the secret of the little slips of paper. It's the law of attraction. It's the contemplation of this accomplishment that actually produces the accomplishment. Don't ask me how it happens, but it does. Say to yourself " I know it, I do it, it's on its way, nothing can stop it and there is nothing to be anxious about."

In Wayne Dyer's book, ***Being in Balance***, he says "the universe is affected by balance, based on the Law of Attraction. He claims you can't attract anything positive when you live in a state of imbalance, complacency, living in fear, and expecting the worse. If you dream it, you can achieve it. That's why writing down your desires on slips of paper really works. You have declared your goal. There have been times when I have completed a book, written down my desire for publication, visualize receiving the acceptance letter in the mail--and it has happened. Just as I visualized it!

Nearly two years ago, my husband, Bob, was diagnosed with IPF which is a rare, genetic, incurable, progressive lung disease. It takes "uncommon courage" for him to face down such a diagnosis, and to greet each day with gratitude. But he does! His lungs fill with fluid and he is subject to violent coughing fits. He has to be very careful of colds or flu and seek immediate medical help. His medication causes stomach pain and loss of appetite and the constant, resultant loss of weight.

In 1997, I wrote an Elf Help gift book called "Gratitude Therapy" which has always helped me; so, I go back to it when I lose my way. He reads it every day! I have published many books which have been read by many adults and children; but that is the most significant "event" that has ever happened to me in my writing career--knowing he reads that book every day.

There's no preparation for such a lethal diagnosis--we all fear it. But how we respond to it is our choice! Bob has chosen to face it head on and take the only powerful medicine he can take to delay the progression. This experimental medicine costs 9,000 dollars a month, which is covered by many different sources--since very few people could carry that financial burden. He takes it religiously every 12 hours even though it causes him to have severe gastric problems. I admire his "uncommon courage" and personal strength.

Bob stays close to God by meditating every day, by not living in constant fear of death, by living "one day at a time" and remembering "There is only God" That takes exceptional "spiritual energy". For now, his disease has been temporally slowed in progression--and we hope for a cure. No one ever knows the future--so we can expect miracles.

Expecting and Experiencing Miracles

Spirituality: A Life Force

In dealing with sickness, we can expect miracles. From a spiritual perspective we are infinite souls, never dying, never born. Our essence is not our material form. When we are faced with a disease in our body, our primary need is to find that spiritual solution.

This generally implies returning our body to a disease-free state as quickly and painlessly as possible. But how can we do this? Aren't we fated to accept cancer or any other terminal disease? Not necessarily! There are many instances of incredible recovery comebacks from what would appear to be a lethal diagnosis. How does this happen? We take full responsibility for any disease or injury saying, "this disease is mine, I own it and I'm in charge of my attitude toward it."

A Course In Miracles makes a revolutionary statement about physical sickness saying it's a defense against the truth. It continues, "sickness is not an accident. Like all defenses, it is an insane device for self-deception. And like all the rest, its purpose is to hide reality, attack it, change it, render it inept, distort it, twist it, and reduce it to a little pile of unassembled parts. The aim of all defenses is to keep the truth from being whole. The parts are seen as if each one were whole within itself." ACIM lesson 136

More simply stated it says if we let our minds harbor attack thoughts, yield to judgments, make plans against uncertainties to come, we have made a decision to be sick. We have misplaced the truth of our spiritual selves, as children of God. Sickness can shield us from the truth that we are healed--a child of God--holy and pure. When we acquire a sense of empowerment and open ourselves up to positive healing energy, we find a spiritual solution. Our bodies respond to this positive energy.

Feeling guilty or angry about heart disease, cancer or any other disease prevents us from reaching the higher levels of energy needed for a miracle. Our whole essence is not our material self. Some believe that there can be a spiritual release of illness, or injury through the individual's personal ability to unite in wholeness with the healing capacity of God. It starts with conceptualizing the mind and body as one; and using our spiritual essence to maintain a sense of perfect unifying health.

The closer we stay to the higher energies--love, kindness, forgiveness, connectedness, gratitude and infinite awareness--leaving behind fear, doubt, hate and separateness, the healthier we will be. Others around us will be healthier too. All illness, metaphysically speaking, is the result of disconnecting our minds and bodies from God.

In **Tears to Triumph**, Marianne Williamson says, "Our problem is that we tend to have more faith in the power of disease to kill us than we have in the power of God to heal us." There is much research today that supports the truth that love can speed the recovery from illness. Doctors who have usually taken a scientific approach are now becoming open to spiritual healing.

Most people in the medical field will not deny the fact that there is some power within the body to heal itself: a power at work that cannot be seen or touched--a spiritual energy. What heals a wound? What keeps our body functioning in perfect harmony? If we're children of God, then we are rooted in spirit. That spirit is perfect. As Wayne Dyer says, "In a sense the body is a manifestation of God's knowledge, an expression of an idea held in the universal consciousness." The body itself is always firmly rooted in the perfection of spirit. But when it loses contact with this perfect spirit, with God, injury or illness can thrive.

Wayne Dyer continues to say, "the intelligence that inhabits your body will become whatever you project it to be. It will create a healthy or sickly body depending on how you choose to use your mind." I believe that somehow there is a mind-body connection that can never be fully understood.

A book by Caroline Myss, Ph.D., called, ***Anatomy of the Spirit: The Seven Stages of Healing*** actually combines scientific medical research with the spiritual to show the correlation. It speaks of spiritual causes of disease and makes a case for holistic healing. Books like these reaffirm what spiritual teachers have known all along. Love does heal!

In ***Embracing The Beloved: Relationship As A Path To Awakening,*** Stephen and Ondea Levine speak from personal experience of the healing exercises they have brought into their marriage. In battling with cancer, and other sickness, they worked together praying as a couple that they might "send forgiveness instead of fear into the pain." They learned to respond to bodily hurt with compassion instead of anger. And it has worked for them.

Couples can come to understand that two hearts can be blended into one healing force. There can be collaboration in healing. No longer is it isolated, individual, but focused on a shared body, and a shared heart. Learning to heal together is one of the divine purposes of a holy relationship.

Some believe the mind-body connection is real and that the God-body connection is the essence of all healing. Healing miracles are not accomplished by asking God to cure us since

God is not withholding his spirit. We seek relief through God by becoming rejoined in the highest spiritual field where God always is. The sense of all healing is to see ourselves as children of God, connected and loved by a higher spiritual energy. Then to work to stay in that space. We rejoin the body with God consciousness.

However, there should never be a sense of failure if a miracle doesn't happen. Life here on earth ends for all of us. The timing is not always ours to understand. If we were able to control the moment of our crossing over to another spiritual level, we would be in charge of all things. This timetable seems to be out of our hands and a mystery we were not meant to understand.

A Course In Miracles further states that when we are healed, we are not healed alone. Sickness is isolation. Healing might be called a "counter-dream" cancelling out the illusion of sickness in the name of truth. Therefore, sickness is an illusion, an unreal dream, which is part of the material world. It claims there is no sickness in the purity of the spirit. The spiritual self will always survive.

Healing is freedom. Healing is shared. Healing is strength. Those who are healed become instruments of healing, like Nancy. They carry healing to the world! And it may not end in a continuation of their physical life as we know it. That is the mystery! If this seems difficult to understand, you're not alone; however, for now we all can feel the spiritual energy, strength and fortitude--the spiritual healing of some around us shining through in the face of pain and loss.

In Wayne Dyer's ***Ten Secrets to Peace and Success***, he explains that there is a universal force that orchestrates everything. We are part of that perfect harmony. We showed up at the right time and we will leave at exactly the right moment. Dyer explains that you and I are an essential part of this complex system: therefore, we must have a purpose. So what is our work, our purpose? What is the work that was placed in our heart when we were born?

I believe it is our intuition that leads us to our purpose. Our intuition is like an invisible companion that nudges us to not waste away another day doing what someone else dictates us to do. If we are "off purpose", we will live with a constant frustration.

Furthermore, Wayne Dyer says, "play the music in your heart so you won't die with it inside you." He continues, "You'll never be at peace if you don't get that music out and let it play. Let the world know why you are here and do it with passion. The passion you feel is God inside you helping you to take the risk to become a spiritual teacher."

Fear and death

Fear of death can drive out our awareness of our spiritual essence. The reality of the spiritual level is formless, timeless and without boundaries. Living in that dimension is living in the realm of wholeness. Understanding that death is unreal-- not nonexistent but unreal, opens the door for Love. In essence, it is Love that is the power that heals.

From *A Course In Miracles* I learned: "There is nothing to fear. The presence of fear is a sure sign you are trusting in your own strength. The awareness that there is nothing to fear shows that somewhere in your mind, though not necessarily a place you recognize yet, you have remembered God, and let His strength take the place of your weakness." The instant I am able to do this I know there is indeed nothing to fear.

Earlier I mentioned Nancy Stevenson who managed to touch the lives of everyone she met as she battled cancer. She did not fear physical death; she feared spiritual death, or a disconnection with God. So, she let her disease take its course while she proclaimed "There is only God". Her defiance of death stayed with her until the moment she left this earth, and her spirit went back to God. Bob and I were with her when she died, along with Joe, her loving husband. It was an honor to have been allowed to witness his love for her and her strength--even in death.

When Doubt Creeps In

But what about those who are plagued with doubts--even about the very existence of God. The world is a fearful place and faith is required to remove fear. You replace fear with faith; and you increase faith by returning to a personal spiritual consciousness of God. You cannot know God through the experiences of others. You can only know God through conscious contact. Being trained in religious beliefs is different from a direct experience of God--"a knowing" that supplies you with faith. It is like riding a bike. You could never know you could ride a bike by someone telling you could. You could only know it by conscious contact with the bicycle-riding itself.

Spirituality: A Life Force

If we come to believe in a power greater than ourselves and have a spiritual awakening, we know there is a God and that faith drives out fear. I came to believe in a higher power when I was a young woman. It struck me that" nothing comes from nothing". I learned in biology about the order of all things, the very intelligence of its function; I learned in botany about the order of the simple tree outside my window; and again was astounded by the very intelligence of its function. Then, in anatomy, I learned about the order of the body and was humbled by the very intelligence of its functioning. In astronomy, I learned about the order of the universe. I came to believe in a higher power. It was simple--there is a higher power of intelligence that is beyond my simple human intelligence--I learned to call that power--God.

Then, when God intervened in my life; I knew that somehow the order of my existence was connected to God. I am a child of God--so when God intervened in my life, I believe "He did for me when I could not do for myself." Healing took place from addiction , from pain, from grief and loss, from fear of death, from insecurities. Miracles happened!

When I wrote the book, ***ABC's of Grief: A Handbook for Survivors***, I had the distinct privilege of being in contact with grieving persons who contributed their poems and stories to my book. What an experience that was! There was Rosemary Gwaltny who chose to be a foster mom for terminally ill children. Besides being a magnificent poet, she was an incredibly faith-filled human being who stared death in the face and won. Here are two of her poems;

Christine A. Adams

Honeysuckle Summer

*Fragrant the
Honeysuckle vines
Behind the back porch
Where we spent the summer
Swinging snugly in the gleaming moonlight.
Barn owls calling urgently
Back and forth. We were lost in each other's
Smiles; hypnotized by each other's hands
Clasped together, in promises of spring.
Entwined in scented dreams sweeter
Than richest masses of blossoms
Twisting yellow through
The railing.
Who could have seen it coming?
The sentence of sickness
Descending.
When the first frost arrived
Lightly dusting pumpkins and squashes,
I lay alone between rows of dried cornstalks
In the field beyond the chicken--house,
Face down in the icy mud
Weeping.*
© by Rosemary J. Gwaltney

In another poem by Rosemary J. Gwaltney, she speaks of her own sense of loss but also states that this poem "could speak for many different people, facing different kinds of losses."

Spirituality: A Life Force

What Can Be Said About Loss
What can be said about loss
In love—
Those gaping wounds bleeding from aching spirits.
Rich libraries of memories calling from those
Cob--webbed shelves of the mind, of empty
Arms, and absent laughter, loving ways,
Sparkling eyes no longer there. Of
Breakfast tables, lonely beds
And favorite things
Gathering
Dust.
What can be said about love
When loss
Rips the tapestry of a spirit apart, leaving threadbare
A soul unraveling. When child, friend, parent, or
Lover carries away with them irretrievably,
A central, vital piece of living. When
Nothing is ever the same again.
When healing takes so very
Long, leaving such
Hideous
Scars.
© by Rosemary J. Gwaltney
www.crossingrivers.com

Christine A. Adams

Signs of the Supernatural

Many people are able to point to the moment of spiritual awakening. The one incredible supernatural sign that let them know God. In this amazing story first published by Centering Corporation in their ***Caring Concepts Newsletter*** (1991), and recounted in my book, ***ABCS of Grief***, Marly Hayer talks about how her faith was restored by an unusual spiritual experience:

"It had been three months since a terrible triple tragedy had befallen us. Our two oldest sons, along with the lovely young girl our eldest had planned to marry, had all died in a house fire at Eastern Illinois University. We were still suffering from shock, incredible grief, and disbelief. Somehow, we managed to go through the motions of the holidays. Now the New Year was here. Reality was sinking in.

We could hardly stand to think of the rest of our lives without our boys. They were honor students, star athletes, and good and loving sons. We were at our lowest ebb.

The night of January 18 was cold and crisp. The stars were bright when I went out for a walk. As I made my way through the darkness, I thought constantly of the three we loved and missed so much. I walked and talked aloud, cried and tried to pray, but it seemed all my former faith and trust were gone. I felt as if I could not go on any longer unless I could be assured that they were all right.

Spirituality: A Life Force

Soon I could not tell if I was shaking from sobs or the cold. I felt as if I just had to know they were safe and happy somewhere. I realized I was freezing cold and utterly exhausted. As I turned to walk back toward the house, something off to the side of the road caught my eye. A bright light seemed to be moving toward me on the left. It was like a very large star. It was low, at the level of the treetops, traveling parallel to the road. It was moving very slowly on a straight path, and not at all like any falling star I had ever seen.

I watched in awe as it kept steadily moving toward me. Then, just as it was directly across and above the spot where I stood, it stopped and broke into three separate stars. They disappeared as quickly as they had come. I was suddenly convinced, beyond a shadow of a doubt, that Bob, Mike, and Carla were with God. I began sensing a peace I had not known for months. A million stars seemed to close in around me. I was overwhelmed with a tremendous feeling of warmth and love and began to weep tears of joy.

My faith was restored. I'm forever grateful for that symbol of light in my darkness. There is no more fear or doubt in my life. Only an unshakable trust that, someday, we will be reunited with our loved ones for all eternity" (by Marly Hayer).

There are many credible stories of persons who have reached beyond the natural world to a supernatural, spiritual place. Sometimes it is the reappearance of someone who has died, sometimes a strange light that appears from nowhere--signs of another supernatural realm--a spirit world. All these signs are too much alike and too frequent to be dismissed.

Christine A. Adams

My final Word

Nancy did die physically. But not spiritually. We were with her when she went back to God. We were there with Joe, her loving husband, and, as I said, it was an honor to witness his love for her and her serenity, the lack of fear, her strength--even in death.

Recently, when it became apparent that a powerful, deadly hurricane was headed towards Florida where we live, my husband, Bob, sensed the danger of Irma. We, like the rest of the U.S. had just witnessed Harvey's destruction in Texas, and it was fresh in Bob's mind. "We have to leave" he declared. I listened even knowing he was dealing with a debilitating lung disease that would make the 1,500 mile trip nearly impossible. Planes were grounded now--we had to drive out of the storm's path.

So even though it was difficult for Bob to breath after any physical exertion, he knew the first thing was to put the heavy aluminum shutters on all windows to save our house. Knowing he couldn't physically close up the house alone he asked me, "Should I call Joe." As he finished the question, his phone rang and identified the number as "Nancy and Joe". An amazing coincidence!

Joe came immediately. They shuttered the house, I packed the car and after a few hours of sleep, at 3AM the next morning we left Florida. It was like someone else was in charge. Joe was not accustomed to call every day. We hadn't spoken to him in a week or more. But, at that very moment, he called; he came and helped Bob with a job that Bob could not physically complete himself in one day. The hurricane intensified and

Spirituality: A Life Force

threatened total destruction in our area as we escaped up the coast.

The next couple of days we drove at night because the roads were clogged with evacuees. We were able to get gasoline and rooms at motels when both were in short supply. Hundreds of people were sleeping in cars at rest areas. Some nights we were there with them!

Ironically, a few days before the hurricane, just as I was celebrating my 82nd birthday and appreciating my general good health, I was tentatively diagnosed with Age Related Macular Degeneration which caused bleeding in my retina. I knew I needed to see a specialist. The retinal bleed was slowly taking my sight in my left eye! On the trip north, I called the Mass Eye and Ear at Mass General in Boston to get help at the Retina Center.

Because I couldn't drive with the bright lights at night, Bob had to take over, driving as many hours as he could. Somehow, we made it--state by state until we got out of the range of Irma. We believe that the warning came from Nancy, through her husband Joe, and she led us out of danger, and to medical help to save my sight. I got into the Retina Emergency Clinic in Boston--and after they deemed the problem "urgent", I received an "intravitreal injection" by a retina specialist and the bleeding began to subside.

Nancy's "spiritual presence" was so powerful in life it's not difficult to believe that her spiritual presence is still here. Nancy always said "There is only God." Whenever, Bob feels the acute physical difficulties of taking the powerful meds, that will hopefully slow his disease, he thinks of Nancy. Whenever she had repeated surgeries, or endless chemotherapy treatments, she could rebound with the realization that the most important thing we have is our spiritual connection to God by always saying "There is only God." Her spirituality was her life force and it has become Bob's, as he struggles to breathe and continue on.

As for me, when Irma's path suddenly swerved, just minutes from our town, I was astounded. What did all this mean? I tried to make sense of our escape from Florida, my escape from continued loss of sight, Bob's ability to make the trip despite a debilitating sickness, and the "near miss" that could have destroyed our house and everything in it!

Then, I pictured in my mind this manuscript, ***Spirituality: A Life Force***, partially edited with its white pages on the floor of my office, with black edit marks on the sides. I saw them destroyed floating in water. We live close to the ocean so it's likely that a direct hit, with storm surge, would have swept up those pages. The only other copy of the manuscript was in my computer on the desk. That could go too! We took all we could with us but decided the computer was too bulky, and too fragile--and I didn't even think to gather the papers on the floor. I had no back-up manuscript with me! To reproduce it would be impossible!

Then, when everything was spared, house, manuscript, original books, I realized the meaning of it all. As we made our way back down the coast, I realized that I have a final writing mission: to use what is left of my eye-sight to complete this book. The overall purpose of this book was to detail my healing transformation from my physical self to the spiritual self. My experience of spirituality as a life force.

A Course In Miracles claims sickness "is a decision to return to our physical self, to turn our minds to our human physical weakness--to a "disease state", when, in truth, we are whole, we are perfect children of God." Healing is freedom! Healing is shared! Healing is strength! And in some strange way, those who are healed, even for an instant, can be instruments of healing, like Nancy and Bob.

I found this quote written in the notes Nancy left behind. "If I have a pearl to give you, it is to accept that change is the most important and sacred thing that there is. Then you are flexible. You have to lie back in the arms of the universe in an attitude of divine nonchalance, because believe me, once you begin to trust, the whole universe changes. You have to trust that happiness is an inevitable outcome of living in these terms. Trust the process and there's no quick fix, so be patient....people get desperate because they are disappointed in their expectations. They've built up an image of where they should be, and when it doesn't work out they are disappointed and they miss out on what is happening." Ann Susskind- Sydney Morning Herald...13/12/1994

The quote above was written in Nancy's handwriting, along with her listings of the medications which she recorded everyday; and the medical notes she took in the doctor's office--but more importantly the many friend's telephone numbers. She never stopped living and loving right until the end. One time she wrote "whatever you want more of, give more of"-- she gave love. And God is Love. So, in her mind there was only God!

As I reach into my eighty-second year of life, writing this book on spirituality, I still have many questions about the mysteries and miracles of life and death. How could I know all that God knows without being equal to God? It's enough for me to know and accept my spiritual transformation as a child of God as I have explained its evolution in this book. If physical sickness comes to me as it has to Nancy and Bob, and as it does to all of us, I pray that my sense of self as a child of God deepens and sustains me--no matter what course my physical self takes. If that is all I have accomplished in my lifetime, it will be enough!

In this last chapter, entitled "Spiritual Energy and Miracles", I look to the "uncommon courage" of my husband Bob, as he maintains his connection to his "spiritual self" even in the face of physical adversity; and I look to Nancy, my friend, whose "spiritual energy" enlightened us all. Both are clearly my most recent "spiritual teachers" teaching me new powerful lessons. **The miracle is that I now carry with me the "uncommon courage " of my husband; and the "enlightened spirit" of Nancy. All I had to do was to be willing to receive it.**

About the Author

Christine A. Adams

Christine A. Adams, M.A., has been writing about issues of addiction, relationships, spirituality, and education for over 35 years. She has over 3,000,000 separate books and pamphlets in print with works published in 54 countries translated into many languages. Christine, an English teacher, was also formerly trained as an addiction counselor in 1986. However, most of her writing parallels her life experiences. Her early writings were about the alcoholic marriage, adult children of alcoholics, teen alcoholism, and sexual addiction. Then came books about spirituality, relationships, grief therapy and education.

In addition, she has produced four very popular Elf Help children's books: <u>Happy To Be Me</u>, <u>Learning To Be A Good Friend</u>, <u>Worry, Worry, Go Away</u>, and <u>God Made Us One By One.</u> One of her best-known recovery books is the adult Elf Help gift book, One Day At A Time Therapy which is still selling in places like Taiwan, China, South Korea, Portugal, the Netherlands, Austria, Sweden, Indonesia, and Brazil.

Among her other books are: Seasons: Spiritual Meditations for Winter, Spring, Summer, and Fall; Let Go, Let God; Teacher of God; Holy Relationships; and ABC's of Grief: A Handbook For Survivors. She has also written a fictional narrative, inspired by her years of teaching, titled The School Factory, as well as a romantic novel named September Love. Additionally, she has authored four out of the five titles in the Spiritual Way of Life series, which encompass Joy, Peace, Love, Acceptance, and Gratitude.

Visit her at www.christineaadams.com or

www.hanleyadamspublishing.com to find all her books.

Also by Christine A. Adams

Peace: A Spiritual Way of Life
Love: A Spiritual Way of Life
Acceptance: A Spiritual Way of Life
Gratitude: A Spiritual Way of Life
Seasons: Spiritual Meditations For Winter, Spring, Summer, and Fall
Spirituality: A Life Force
ABC's of Grief – A Handbook for Survivors
Let Go and Let God
Teacher of God
Holy Relationships
Living in Love
September Love
Claiming Your Own Life
School Factory
Love, Infidelity, and Sexual Addiction
Gratitude Therapy
One Day At A Time
Learning To Be A Good Friend
Happy To Be Me
Worry, Worry, Go Away
God Made Us One By One

Thank you for reading **Spirituality: A Life Force!** I hope you enjoyed it as much as I enjoyed writing it. If you did, I would be grateful if you could take a moment to leave a review on the site where you bought this book, or go to https://www.goodreads.com and share any thoughts or information you would care to leave about this book. Reviews are incredibly helpful for authors and also help other readers discover new books.

Here is a sample of "**Living In Love: Connecting to the Power of Love Within**"

Thank you for your support and happy reading!

Christine A. Adams

Living In Love

Connecting To The

Power of Love Within

Christine A. Adams

Introduction

Most of my childhood and early adulthood were spent dealing with loss. I did not think about spiritual progress because I was preoccupied with surviving. Through the years alcoholism had disrupted my life and the life of my family, creating dysfunction that left me ill-equipped to deal with my future. When I was fourteen years old, my father died leaving my mother with eight children from ages two to fourteen. I was devastated.

After attending a Catholic college, where religion rather than spirituality was taught, I began my search for self in accomplishments, money and marriage. Alcoholism destroyed my marriage as it had plagued my family of origin. It nearly killed me. Alcoholism cheated our children of family unity and left them to cope with problems peculiar to adult children of alcoholics. Finally I left that marriage and admitted that I could no longer drink in safety.

At forty years of age I joined a 12-Step program that changed my life by promoting a physical, mental and spiritual recovery. Physically I withdrew from alcohol and all mind-altering substances each day, one day at a time. Attended 12-Step meetings and associated with other recovering alcoholics who could help me in my recovery. The obsession with alcohol left me. The losses stopped and, for the first time in my life, I began to move forward to gain new physical health, new clarity of mind and anew feeling of self-worth. This was just the end of the beginning.

Getting Honest With Myself

In the first year I found myself alone bringing up three teenagers. It was a fight for survival and I felt frightened, desperate and ashamed. Nevertheless I had surrendered to God, knowing I couldn't go it alone any longer. There was no place for me to go so I turned to the people in the 12-Step programs and asked for help. They told me to pray, to practice the 12 Steps and to hang on. I did as they said. At the end of that year, I got a sponsor and did a Fourth Step inventory of my life which I shared with my sponsor.

The next two years were spent dealing with the knowledge gained by that Fourth Step inventory. With the encouragement of my sponsor I began to get honest with myself and admit to my most glaring defects of character. Slowly I did as Step 6 advises and asked God to remove these defects. My mind began to clear. During these years went back to school taking 43 credit hours in alcohol and drug-counseling courses. This knowledge became the basis for my writing and a foundation for my sobriety. I had settled my account with the disease of alcoholism by staying sober and learning about it. There was no doubt in my mind about the deadly, insidious power of addiction after these studies. If my own denial ever allowed me to minimize the significance of my own disease, my coursework reminded me that addiction kills and that if I ever lose sight of the power of addiction it will kill me. It took learning, coupled with my own experience and that of others, to free me mentally from any reservations about addiction. I knew I could never use alcohol and other drugs safely. I had taught English composition and combined my professional expertise with my knowledge of addiction to begin a writing career.

Other Dependencies

In the fourth year of my recovery I began a co-dependent relationship in which my partner became my addiction. Although I felt the need for a committed relationship, I did not know that adult children of alcoholics have issues that need to be attended to before they enter into commitment. I began to attend ACoA meetings just as I entered this brief second marriage. When I discovered I had married a man with an active sexual addiction — a need to have affairs with other women — I realized our marriage was inoperative and left. My first book on adult children of alcoholics was published shortly after this unhealthy relationship ended.

Darkness To Light

Years six and seven were dark and desperate times for me as I discovered how devastating co-dependency is. I began my spiritual recovery at this point. My decision to file for divorce precipitated a time of turmoil and confusion. But out of this struggle came the beginning of my recovery from co-dependency.

I learned that co-dependency is a spiritual issue that stems from a lack of spiritual wholeness. I began to experience more honesty, more growth, more understanding about other dependencies that destroy lives. I began to write about sexual addiction and co-addiction. In the eighth and ninth years I was faced with surviving the loss of a marriage and the terrible shame and social censure that co-addiction had brought into my life. It left me shaken. I had to look carefully at myself and at all of my relationships. Patiently

Spirituality: A Life Force

I read, learned and wrote about co-dependency. My second major book was published at this time.

Some unusual circumstances within my marriage led me back to organized religion. A small ray of light came through as I practiced my religion and found solace. For the first time, religious practices offered me spiritual growth. A new spiritual awareness developed and began to break through the darkness.

More Light

In years ten and eleven of my recovery, I started attending meetings to study *A Course In Miracles* at my church. It is a self-taught course in spiritual transformation. Because these meetings were held immediately before the Sunday morning service, they were easy to fit into my schedule. Even though I still attended 12-Stepmeetings during the week, I thought *A Course In Miracles* might give me an added spiritual dimension. I had no idea the three volumes of the course would so profoundly change my perspective, move me to peace and commit me to love. At first I just considered it a part of my church program. Then it became much more. By helping me to get out of the victim role of the recently divorced co-dependent, it showed me that forgiveness was a gift tome. It personalized my conscious contact with God and gave me the spiritual strength and support I needed to live. As I began to learn the *Course,* I found myself unable to record my experience in writing. In those early years the ideas just washed over me and cleansed me.

Spiritual Changes

In the thirteenth and fourteenth years of recovery, new spiritual awareness grew through my continued study of *A Course In Miracles.* The first and most profound change came when I accepted the teaching, "I am a child of God." After that idea became internalized, I began to discover how to live as a child of God. My behavior gradually changed as I was released from old ego-centered, co-dependent patterns. I embraced discipline and saw it as a vehicle for joy in my life. Prayer became sacred and coveted, God was closer now and I was no longer afraid. Others noticed changes in me and wondered where I got my sense of peace. They asked me what it meant to be a child of God. They asked me how to get peace of mind. Slowly, I began to record disjointed phrases and ideas but it did not yet evolve into a pattern.

Glorious New Beginnings

Spirituality: A Life Force

Finally I no longer felt the need to people-please. I started being totally honest, telling the real truth, setting boundaries and living freely as myself. The first signs of healthy relationships began to emerge as I became present for them. It became okay to be alone, to be in or out of an intimate relationship with a man. It meant loving all people, not just special people. My view of my surroundings, my actions and my reactions changed. This change in perspective has left me open to people in my life and, more importantly, open to God. Out of these perceptions came the framework for *Living In Love*. It is only a beginning for me, but I know it is the most glorious beginning of my life. It is my hope that my words and experiences assist you with new beginnings as you move forward in your own spiritual recovery.

Chapter 1 - You Are A Child Of God

You Are A Child Of God

1

No matter where you are in life, no matter what is happening, you are always doing the best you can do with the knowledge and awareness you have. You are perfect just the way you are. There is no timetable and you can't progress too slowly or too quickly. You are perfect in your imperfection. You are always a child of God.

Christine A. Adams

Do you sometimes think you are not enough? Do you tell yourself that you are not smart enough? Not attractive enough? Not good enough? If you have the vague sense of not being "enough," you are not alone.

Many psychological difficulties — anxiety, underachievement in school, emotional immaturity, sexual dysfunction, chronic spells of depression — can be attributed to low self-esteem. Many people suffer from insecurity, self- doubt, and guilt, and are afraid to participate fully in life.

In his book, *How To Raise Your Self-Esteem*, Nathaniel Branden says, "How we feel about ourselves crucially affects virtually every aspect of our existence ... as our responses to events are shaped by who and what we think we are." Branden continues, "The tragedy is that so many people look for self-confidence and self-respect everywhere except within themselves and so they fail in their search." He goes on to describe positive self-esteem as a kind of "spiritual attainment."

Usually thinking you are not enough is a spiritual issue. It disavows the existence of the spiritual self and indicates you are relying on human powers alone, not the power and presence of God. Thinking you are not enough *indicates* a lack of faith and a misunderstanding of your true nature as a child of God.

One of the reasons for not accepting our spiritual selves might be own lack of forgiveness. In our human frailty, we all err. Yet, if we can't get beyond our mistakes, we may never see our spiritual selves — that is, the forgiven child of God. Self-esteem is the reputation we acquire with ourselves. When we remember only our mistakes, see only our frailties and picture ourselves as sinful, we cannot find that child of God within.

It is in our internalized conviction as children of God that we finally see that we are enough; in fact, we are holy, chosen ones. It is in our connection with God, with love itself, that we learn to love ourselves and live in the power and glory of God's love. It is true that we are never enough in ourselves, but in the light of our inheritance as God's children and in the light of God's Love, we are everything, we are whole, we are perfect, and we are enough.

If I could say only one thing to you, I would say, "You are a child of God." Then again and again, "You are a child of God." For me, coming to believe that I am a child of God was the most important transformation of my life. It meant a re-imaging of self. Once this was accomplished a change in self-esteem quickly followed.

But how does one become a child of God? By becoming willing to change and let God make the transformation. By letting Him into our lives.

When I started the 12-Step program, I kept hearing the words of the Third Step, "Came to believe that a Power greater than ourselves could restore us to sanity." For me, finding that Power meant returning to childhood, getting in touch with my inner child and then getting in touch with my Creator.

The first thing I did was to search for a picture of myself as a child. When I found it and positioned it on the shelf, I realized that if God is in me now, He was also there within that child. What a healing realization. Truly I was not just a child of this world, not solely of my parents, but a child of God.

This single experience enabled me to begin learning about my inner child, to reach back and remember her as she really was. It was at this point that I started letting God in to heal her within me. My task became to attend to that child's needs, to change the negative messages given to her, and to re-image that child into God's child.

Sometimes I was easily led back to an image of myself as "less than." I returned to seeking perfection, needing love while feeling unlovable, seeking control while feeling out of control and looking for security in an unsafe world. Often, I returned to the old patterns, feeling feelings I thought I was not supposed to feel, seeking acceptance, and not knowing I am acceptable, desiring maturity but remaining that child. The transformation began when I first acknowledged, without blaming my parents, the neglect that child had known. Then I nurtured that child, and, finally, changed my perspective. Ultimately, I knew that, in reality, I am in God and with God — God's child.

It was a matter of finding the perspective of faith — the coming to believe. God did not make us to abandon us. He did not intend us to view ourselves and our environment with distrust. God made us to be His children and promised us His unconditional love and care. This thought emerges again and again in A Course In Miracles:

- I am sustained by the Love of God.
- As I listen to God's voice, I am sustained by His Love.
- As I open my eyes, His Love lights up the world for me to see.

- As I forgive, His Love reminds me that His Son is sinless.
- And as I look upon the world with the vision, He has given me, I remember that I am His Son.

The essence of the Course's teachings is the concept that the Divine breaks through from love itself into each life. Thus, each person represents a spark of the Divine and is interconnected with all creation. That perception of each of us as a child of God helps us to see our mission in life clearly and to let go of the fear that destroys the love we generate from within.

With my change in perception came a change in the negative messages that had controlled me since childhood. In my recovery from alcoholism, there was a spiritual awakening. My shame was replaced with respect, and the new child was prompted to emerge. In recovery, I learned that God is the one who can sustain the positive messages.

I need to hear. This reversal from the negative to positive helped me to re-image myself as a child of God. Then when A Course In Miracles reiterated those ideas, I was ready to hear.

My journal entry at that time more clearly details the process:

> I've become aware of the power of God within me. It is the growing consciousness, and I need to keep in contact with that power. His power can put me above selfish pettiness; it can move me in directions I would not dare move otherwise. His power can sustain me through the pain of any loss.

Christine A. Adams

I've come to believe that the most important ingredient in my life is the power of God within. It will be my sustaining force until I return to Him. Those who love me will not sustain me, nor will the material possessions that make me comfortable make me whole. Only that power of love within me that I call God can sustain me without fail.

Through the years I've tried to experience my own sense of power in other persons, in position and in things — and that would sustain me for a while. Eventually, though, that connection would dim. I then returned again and again to the spirit within where I found the power of God. That power never dims.

Today, when I am troubled by others who would harm me, I think of this power of God within me, and I know I am loved. If I try to protect myself from all harm, I will be ineffective. But if I let God protect and guide me, I know I'll be cared for. God is a safe new place.

When we look outside ourselves for our identity we are bound to fail. The world is far too transient. When we look inside, claiming our rightful spiritual identity as a child of God, we are bound to see our true selves.

Low self-esteem is a spiritual issue. It is bound up with our inability to see that which is within us, our inability to connect with the perfection within our imperfect human body, to connect with our souls.

Spirituality: A Life Force

"I Am Lovable"

The first negative message that changed for me was "I am not lovable." If I am of God, of Love itself, then that meant "I am lovable." God loves me unconditionally.

When I re-imaged myself as a child of God, I emerged as a less needy, more loving person. No longer did I depend solely on others for affection, attention, and love. I de- pended on God. My happiness in a relationship was no longer the responsibility of my partner. What a burden! What an unrealistic expectation! I was no longer con- trolled by others, led out of myself and torn away from my own center of peace and serenity. Unhealthy co-dependence had always led me away from God because I believed that in and of myself, I was not lovable. It would take my partner's love to make me lovable, not my self- love to keep me whole.

Other very important issues were brought to light with this new perspective. If I am of Love itself, then I have the right to be treated in a loving way and the responsibility to maintain self-love and discipline. No longer could I allow abuse in my life. No longer could I live without the dignity due a child of God. So, I set limits in relationships, communicated my needs in a loving way, no longer feared abandonment and refused to accept physical or psychological abuse.

When I accept myself as God's child, I see myself as loved and loving, as perfect in my imperfection. There is joy in that recognition. Great joy.

When The Student Is Ready,

The Teacher Comes

Whenever I need a teacher, God puts one in my life. This time it came through my classroom in the form of one of my students, a lovely young woman named Rebecca.

On the first day of class the students seemed edgy and concerned. It became clear they were angry about Rebec- ca, who was not present for the class.

"I don't care, I'm glad we told," Melinda whispered.

"Are you sure she won't be in big trouble?" another asked.

"She is already in big trouble!" Melinda quickly interjected.

It was clear that this class was not going to function until Rebecca got there. The door opened and an attractive blond hurriedly entered the room, taking her place in the circle. A tense silence gripped the room.

"They are trying to tell me what to do," she said aloud. No one dared to speak. As if in mockery of the serious- ness in the room, the chorus next door started to sing. Rebecca took that as a signal to begin as she shuffled in her chair and opened her book. Everyone watched her and did the same.

Rather than going on with this tense, distracted class, I decided to challenge Rebecca.

"Who is trying to do this, Rebecca?" I asked.

"They think I jumped in front of Bill's car intentionally last night," she answered. For the first time, I noted the scratches on her face and arms.

"My parents want to put me away," she said disgustedly. "It's that Student Assistance Team — they think I'm crazy," she went on. The rest of the class reacted with concern and sympathy. Rebecca was their friend.

Very quickly I realized that as a teacher I was in risky territory and tried to defuse the situation by saying that each case is individual and that the team might not be right in every case.

"I don't know your situation, Rebecca," I added.

With that the class slowly moved to begin the lesson. The next day the principal called me into his office.

"I got a call from Rebecca Howard's parents last night and they were furious," he said a bit agitated.

"What happened?"

"Did you tell Rebecca that the Student Assistance Team was wrong in her case?"

"Never," I said emphatically, realizing that Rebecca had taken what I said out of context. The moment I realized how desperate and how clever Rebecca had been, I became angry.

The principal explained further that Rebecca used what I said out of context in the emergency meeting at the psychiatrist's office at a local hospital yesterday afternoon. She was building her case so that she might not be hospitalized for her self-inflicted wounds. She was determined to stay with her boyfriend whom she was obsessively attached to.

I had to face her the next day. At first, I felt used and betrayed, but eventually I recognized that her desperate actions sprang from a sad and lonely place inside. I decided not to confront her but to help her and be there for her.

When I got to know Rebecca, I recognized that she was suffering from co-dependency in its most severe form. She really believed that if Bill left her, she would die. Bill was charming, captivating and controlling, and in her mind, she thought she did not have enough of herself to make it without him.

It was a long, dangerous year for me and for Rebecca. With each crisis, I listened. Having just ended a destructive co-dependent situation in my own life, I could relate. Rebecca became my teacher. She became an example of the dangers of thinking you are not enough, of believing that someone else holds your life in their hands. I talked her through many days when she did not see how she could go on.

"You are a fine writer, Rebecca, the best in the class," I told her. She heard only partially because her mind was always on Bill. Then slowly she began to gain strength. I think she knew that I had suffered through co-dependency and was making my way out of it. We leaned on each other for a year until she graduated. She and Bill may still be together, but Rebecca is a stronger person today. She no longer chooses to harm herself when he retracts his love because she has developed her own sense of worth. God always sends me a teacher when I am the most in need. Rebecca was one of the best.

"I Am Safe"

The second negative message that changed for me was, "I am not safe." If I am of God, of love itself, then, "I am safe!" At all times, the love of God will keep me safe and guide me. Even though I continue to see tragedy and sickness around me, the world has become spiritually safe for me because God is my parent, my protector.

I have learned to listen to my inner self in order to discern what might be dangerous. When I sense danger, I look to God for the courage to proceed. Bad things do not elude me, but my perspective has changed.

I first initiated trust in my life by developing trust in God. Then it spilled over into relationships with others. Over and over again, I turned my life and will over to the care of God as I understood Him; and, over and over again, He did not fail me.

As long as I remember "God's will for me is joy," I can accept seemingly unfortunate situations. Many times, I did not know the results of some loss until long after it had occurred, but I knew that God would never abandon me and that in time I would see some good from a seemingly bad situation.

Just this week I was reminded of this truth again. Jennifer Hodges, the daughter of a close friend of mine, was killed in a helicopter crash. Jennifer was the nurse on the Life Star helicopter that rescues accident victims and carries them to Hartford Hospital, Connecticut.

Ironically, she was killed trying to rescue someone. Her death shocked and moved thousands of people. On the night of the wake, I stood in line for four hours with thousands of others outside the funeral home. It started to rain. The hundreds of emergency medical technicians, firefighters and policemen in line took out plastic garbage bags. They handed them back through the line and we covered our heads. Lightning flashes cut the sky and the rain poured down, yet no one went home. We all stayed in line, inching our way into the funeral home. Five thousand of us!

When I finally reached Jennifer's father, a deeply spiritual man, he hugged me and said the most remarkable thing.

"Some good will come out of this. You will see, Chris. You will see."

I could not think of one good thing at the time.

The next day the memorial and burial service was held at a large city church that could seat only a fraction of the thousands who wanted to get in. A sound system carried the words of tribute from Jennifer's coworkers to the crowd. Parents whose children had been saved by Jennifer and Life Star wept on the lawn, children whose parents had been saved wept as well.

When Jennifer's cremated body was placed in the earth, the Life Star helicopter passed over the church. There wasn't a dry eye in the crowd.

Some might see no logic in Jennifer's death. She was so young and dedicated, so vital in her work, helping to save this man's daughter, that man's son. How could I really agree with her father and see anything good in her death? At that moment, it seemed difficult.

On reflection, however, I realized there was great holiness in the outpouring of love at the time of Jennifer's death. Those thousands of people who work to help others were united in one place at one time to honor someone who believed in love and lived in love.

Never could I have re-created a more profound example of living in love than what I saw at Jennifer's funeral. At the interment, the Life Star helicopter passed over the gravesite as a reminder that her loving service will continue.

At that moment, it was clear that Jennifer's death had great meaning. She did not die uselessly. Her love went on in the renewed dedication of every service person there. Her love continued on in each mission of that helicopter and in each loving act of her colleagues.

Love is like that — it does not end with the giver. Love flows on to the next person and the next and the next. Love brings more love.

"I Am Okay"

The third negative message that changed for me was "I am not okay." As a child of God, this message no longer fit. It became "I am okay."

As a child I felt unacceptable, and I would invariably try harder, striving for perfection in all areas of my life. If I were perfect, I had a chance of forging order out of the disorder in my life. Ultimately, it became clear to me that perfectionism didn't work. It was only through my connection with God that I could be okay. When I understood that I am God's child, not God, I could accept my limitations and failings.

Accepting our true selves creates a paradox by asking us to forgive ourselves our human frailties on the one hand and to view ourselves as perfect spiritual beings on the other. Only when we see through this seeming contradiction, and rid ourselves of trying to be perfect, can we come to love ourselves.

When we can come to understand ourselves as perfect spiritual beings, or children of God, we are ready to love ourselves as God loves us. It would be hard to conceive of the energy of God as a conditional force, one that picks and chooses its subjects to love. Therefore, we are asked to forgive ourselves our imperfections and love ourselves unconditionally. Is that easy? Not always. But it's ever so necessary for peaceful, positive, and powerful living.

Louise L. Hay writes in The Power Is Within You, "We usually make loving ourselves conditional, and then when we are involved in relationships, we make loving the other person conditional also."

So it is that we find it difficult to love another until we love ourselves. Here are some simple rules for loving yourself:

1 Be gentle with yourself

Everything takes time. Therefore, give yourself the time you need to love yourself. When you forgive yourself, you lift a great weight off your shoulders. All of us are at exactly the place we need to be at any given moment. Give yourself permission to grow and to come to the awareness of life. What is your hurry? Be kind, but not indulgent. Be kind to yourself. You are God's child.

2 Be kind to your mind

Fill your mind with positive affirmations. You are worth it. Don't abuse your precious mind with negative thoughts and digressions. Say nice things to yourself every day. Begin with the words, "I am God's precious child." Be kind to your mind by praying, meditating, reading positive words and visualizing positive outcomes.

3 Stop criticizing yourself

Loving ourselves means that we don't beat ourselves up by telling ourselves that we are bad or dumb or worthless. Stop mercilessly judging yourself. There is nothing wrong with you. You are God's child.

4 Stop scaring yourself

Sometimes we carry around a sense of impending doom. Let it go! You do not need to be afraid. Fears of abandonment and rejection are not real, so stop scaring yourself. There is nothing to fear when you rely on the love and power of God.

5 Praise yourself

Don't listen to your own negative defamations. Give them up in favor of positive affirmations of praise. Tell yourself, "I am wonderful." Not just once, but all the time. You are a wonderful child of God. Praise your strengths and accomplishments. If you can do it for even one minute at a time, it will help. Talk to yourself as a loving God would talk to His child.

6 Accept all things as good and be grateful

So often we see only the negative side in an event or happening. Look for the positive side. Ask yourself, "What is the lesson which I must learn?" Look for it and be grateful.

Life's paradoxes often weave intricate patterns of forgiveness for us. I once found myself needing to forgive myself for betraying a trusted friend. That mistake stayed with me and I never fully forgave myself.

Then a trusted friend betrayed me in exactly the same way I had betrayed my friend. I was filled with a hatred and rage, which I thought I'd never release.

After a long, desperate struggle with anger and grief, I realized this woman had been my teacher. She had given me a precious gift. She became the vehicle for me to give forgiveness and, ultimately, to experience God's forgive- ness for myself. I knew that if I could forgive her, I could see myself as washed clean of the harm I had once done to my friend.

I knew I'd found a special key in that experience. Now when I think of the woman who harmed me, I smile. Through her betrayal I attained a great personal victory.

Christine A. Adams

"I Am In Control"

The fourth negative message transformed in me was, "I am not in control," which became, "I am in control." Until this realization took hold I had wavered back and forth between trying to exert unreasonable control over people, places and things and abdicating, giving up control completely. My behavior was oppressive, disruptive, and confusing.

Finally, I realized the only thing that I could reasonably control was myself. All other attempts were futile and frustrating. For the truth is, no matter what we fear, no matter what is at stake, we are not in control of much in life except our happiness, our personal behavior, the way we treat and think about ourselves and others. That is enough. All else is in God's hands.

As God's children, we will not be abandoned even when things seem impossibly out of control. In times of crisis, we need to consciously turn our lives, and the circum- stances of our lives, over to God. We are responsible only for ourselves.

If my children drink abusively, it is not my responsibility; they are in control of their own actions. If my husband is unfaithful, it is not my responsibility; he is in control of his own actions. If I am subject to someone's jealousy or anger, it is not my responsibility; I am not in control of others' feelings. If someone is irresponsible, it is not my responsibility; others are responsible for their own irresponsibility. If someone is intolerant of me, it is not my responsibility; they are in control of their own attitudes.

All we can possibly control in any situation is our own thinking and behavior, the choices we make. If we listen to internal negative messages and choose negative behaviors, we could meet infidelity with infidelity or drunken- ness with drunkenness or anger with anger. We could be intolerant or irresponsible.

Or we can take care of ourselves and guard our own actions in the sight of God. We can decide to live in love. Others have to be responsible for their relationships with themselves and God, just as I am responsible for my relationship with myself and God. God knows what is best for others as he knows what is best for me. If I allow Him to be God, I won't deem it necessary, or even desirable, to control others.

With this in mind, we can erase any negative message from childhood that says, "I am not in control," and replace it with, "I am in control." Tending to ourselves and to our relationship with God ultimately allows us to experience ourselves as being fully in control.

"I Will Always Be Helped And Protected"

The fifth negative message to be changed was, "I will not be helped and protected," which became, "I will always be helped and protected."

If we experience ourselves as children of God, we know we are not alone. We will be helped. All we need do is ask — and have faith that our answers will come. God can and will steer us toward the proper decisions. In His love, he can and will show us what steps to take. He can and will help us to maintain our self-respect, dignity, and values. There are no broken promises or lies with God, just truth and love. We can rest assured that all answers lie within us if we just ask for help to see them.

A Course In Miracles repeats this idea many times and in many ways:

God is my strength. Vision is His gift. You will see because it is the Will of God.

As we know the help and protection of God, there will be an integration of self, a "making whole" and a sense of spiritual well-being that comes over us. Because we have changed our perspective, we no longer see ourselves as fearful. We are safe.

In the final stage of my re-imaging of myself, the negative message, "I have little faith," became, "I have great faith in God and God is the love in which I live."

During this process, I was moved to a greater sense of my true self, to my true spiritual depth. My spiritual life, my union with God as His child, is personal. I have discovered faith in my own way and time just as you are finding it now.

My faith has become useful in my day-to-day life, providing basic ingredients for living: trust, freedom, and joy. It's experiential, like 12-Step work and A Course In Miracles.

Though words cannot explain fully the meaning of being a child of God, it is possible to accept the truth of it in the center of your being. You can break out of all your old images of yourself and into a new, more spiritual self. One of love itself.

The old message, "I have little faith in God," becomes "I have great faith in God." Gradually you realize that your faith in God is not only your greatest treasure, it is all you need.

www.ingramcontent.com/pod-product-compliance
Lightning Source LLC
Chambersburg PA
CBHW052021070526
44584CB00016B/1843